Dr Greg
Asheville
Hewitt

Stepping in the Stream
learning to relate
to the will of God

Also by Beth Crissman

Longing to Belong:
Learning to Relate as the Body of Christ

Feeding and Leading of Shepherds:
Learning to Relate as Sheep and Shepherds

October 19, 2017

November 1, 2006

Stepping in the Stream

learning to relate to the will of God

To Susan:

Beth M. Crissman

Prayers written by Debbie Gunter

[signature]

PLOWPOINT

Breaking Ground for the Seed of the Gospel

Stepping in the Stream: Learning to Relate to the Will of God

ISBN-10: 0-9762277-3-8
ISBN-13: 978-0-9762277-3-1

Published by Plowpoint Press of Graham, North Carolina.
Book Manufactured by Edwards Brothers of Ann Arbor, Michigan and Lillington, North Carolina.

For permissions or more information please contact:
Plowpoint
PO Box 979
Graham, NC 27253
(336)226-0282
www.plowpoint.org

Publisher's Cataloging-in-Publication
(Provided by Quality Books, Inc.)
Crissman, Beth M.
    Stepping in the stream : learning to relate to the will of God / Beth M. Crissman.
        p. cm. -- (Relation transformation series ; 3)
        Includes bibliographical references.
        LCCN 2006902800   ISBN 0-9762277-3-8   ISBN 0-9762277-5-4
    1. Christian life. 2. Discernment (Christian theology) 3. God--Will.
    I. Title. II. Series.
BV4509.5.C74 2006   248.4   QBI06-600133

Dedication

To the faithful sojourners at
Berry Temple United Methodist Church and
Covenant Community United Methodist Church
who chose to
step in the stream with us.

Contents

Trust in the Lord
with all your heart;
do not depend
on your own
understanding.
Seek his will
in all you do,
And he will direct
your paths.
Proverbs 3:5-6

Introduction

Before You Begin

*W**hen* you set out on any journey, it's important to know how you're going to get there and what you need to take along. *Stepping in the Stream* is a guide for a journey—your faith journey of discerning God's purpose for your life and your ministry. Through this guide, you will explore the difference between setting your own course for the journey (strategic planning) and discerning and submitting to the strategic vision set for you by God. Through strategic planning, you would focus on implementing your best ideas. Through *Stepping in the Stream*, you will learn first how to discern the difference between your good ideas and God's ideas and then how to pursue passionately the latter.

Stepping in the Stream is written to be used as a group exercise but it is also useful for an individual's personal discernment of call. The key to its use, however, is to engage the content as a prayerful process of clarifying God's mission, vision, and purpose for you and your ministry. The book itself is written as an unfolding process with

> *This is a guide for your faith journey to discern God's purpose in your life and ministry*

each chapter building on what was learned previously. The overall process includes reviewing your own history, practicing the spiritual disciplines, developing a relational covenant, conducting needs assessments and demographic studies, discovering your spiritual gifts and passions, and developing specific strategies to put God's vision into action.

Each chapter also includes questions for discussion and practical "Next Steps" to be applied directly in your ministry. Additionally, daily scripture readings and prayer guides are offered at the end of each chapter to keep you *in the stream* with God and *in step* with one another throughout the process. On the pages with the daily readings and prayers, we have also provided areas for you to make "Focus Notes" of how God may be speaking to you and how you may be speaking to God.

For optimal group effectiveness, participants should read each chapter before gathering together so your time can be focused primarily on the group exercises. In this way, *Stepping in the Stream* will become a useful guide for a ministry team, church staff, or other leadership to discern and apply God's vision directly to your ministry area.

When engaged as a group process, we also encourage you to allow time for a simple, common meal and for personal sharing. In doing so, you will be simultaneously nurtured in mind, body, and spirit as God prepares you to go forth and nurture others.

Discerning God's will for our lives and ministries is a lifelong journey of faith. Get ready to take the right next steps *in the stream* so God can take you where God desire you to go.

Special Instructions

At the end of each chapter, there is a special section entitled "The Right Next Step" which includes activities to apply the content of *Stepping in the Stream* directly to your ministry by the next time you gather. Please take note that the activities in the following chapters may require additional time or preparation:

- **Page 54: preparing a timeline or history of your ministry or church to review together when you gather for Chapter Three "Weaving Our Stories with THE Story."**

- **Page 120: conducting demographic surveys and needs assessment interviews of your "neighbors" (or the people to whom you are called to serve) when you gather for Chapter Six "Hearing the Cries of the Needy."**

- **Page 138: obtaining and distributing a spiritual gifts inventory to be completed by all members of the group and compiled to review when you gather for Chapter Seven "Finding Your Burning Bush."**

Trust in the Lord
with all your heart;
do not depend
on your own
understanding.
Seek his will
in all you do,
And he will direct
your paths.
Proverbs 3:5-6

One

Joining the Journey

At some point in every person's life and in the life of every church, we stop and ask ourselves, "Where do we go from here?" Rather than coming up only once, this question emerges time and time again. In fact, our lives and our ministries are an unfolding journey marked by various intersections along the way, and at each critical turning point we are faced again with the question:

Where do we go from here?

Several years ago, I was serving two very different congregations, and yet both churches were faced with critical turning points in their ministries. One church was less than ten years old with a fast-growing, younger congregation. The other church was over one hundred years old whose multiracial congregation represented rich history and experience. And yet, despite the apparent differences in demographics, resources, and locations, these two churches shared a common place on their journeys marked by common questions.

At many points on our faith journey, we ask the question: Where do we go from here?

As a pastor and shepherd to these two congregations, I often fretted, even struggled, about what we should do next. I wanted so much to lead these congregations along God's right path for them, but many days I felt clueless regarding the next steps to take.

One night, in the midst of my fretting, I awakened to a clear message of direction regarding the right next step. I simply heard, "Beth, step into the stream." I got up and began to pray and ask for clarity when I sensed the Lord revealing this image of the stream as illustrative of God's will. It seemed to me that God was saying, "If you will focus on getting into the stream of my will, I will take you where you need to go."

> *Trust in the Lord with all your heart;*
> *do not depend on your own understanding.*
> *Seek his will in all you do,*
> *and he will direct your paths.*
>
> **Proverbs 3:5-6 NLT**

Doing Good Things or Doing God-Things

Now, for those of us who are very accustomed, and even comfortable, in making things happen on our own, this idea of someone else directing our path can be a bit unsettling. After all, we have a lot of good ideas, and we can see a lot of things that need to get done. And yet, the distinction is this:

We can do a lot of "good things" or we can do the "God-things" God desires us to do.

Only by doing the "God things" will we be co-laborers with Jesus to bring about the Kingdom of God in our midst. Not only did Jesus teach us that he will bring the Kingdom of God in the fullness of time, but that we are invited to participate in bringing about the Kingdom here and now!

> *Once Jesus was asked by the Pharisees when the kingdom of God was coming, and he answered, "The kingdom of God is not coming with things that can be observed; nor will they say, 'Look, here it is!' or 'There it is!' For, in fact, the kingdom of God is among you."* **Luke 17:20-21 NRSV**

The Kingdom of God is among us each time we actively allow God into our lives. When we allow God's powerful presence in us, through us, and among us the Kingdom is present. This is what it means for us to pray as Jesus taught:
   Your Kingdom come. Your will be done on earth as it is in heaven.

But too often, we busy ourselves with lots of "good things" to do, but we fail to commit ourselves to doing the "God things" that would bring about the Kingdom of God in our very midst. To do the God-things, the message and the mandate remain clear:

Step into the Stream.

The wisdom of Proverbs calls us to do just that—to take the one right next step by stepping into the will of God and trusting that God alone knows where we need to go and what we need to do. Therefore, the one right next step is to step into the stream of God's will and to allow God to direct our paths.

Stepping into the stream is a process of discerning and submitting to God's will. It is a journey of faith that is marked by our trusting God to take us where we need to go. The writer of Hebrews reminds us in chapter eleven, verse one that faith is… *the confident assurance that what we hope for is going to happen. It is the evidence of things we cannot see.*

> *To do the "God-things" we must Step into the Stream of God's will.*

When we step into the stream of God's will, we relinquish control of the destination, and we trust God to direct the steps of how we will get there.

The Journey Is Our Destination

Since the beginning of time and our taking leave from the Garden of Eden, we have become a people on the move in search of our ultimate home. In fact, the biblical story is a travel journal of the people of God on an incredible journey. Throughout Christian history, the life of the Church, at its best, can be described as a movement that emerged from the followers of "The Way." We are part of a movement that began thousands and thousands of years ago that, by God's grace, is still on the move.

As believers, we are part of a journey that began thousands of years ago.

And yet we live in a world that tells us to "settle down" and to "make ourselves at home" when our "real home" is another world away. If we are truly discerning and yearning for the Kingdom of God, then we must admit that we are not there yet, and we will not stop until we get there.

Several years ago, my family set out on a three week camping trip across the United States. Less than six hours into the trip, our children asked the predictable question:

"Are we there yet?"

In response to this anticipated and often dreaded question, my husband, Kelly, responded with much enthusiasm, "This is it! We're there! The trip is our destination!" With great wisdom, Kelly set the tone for what was truly an incredible and memorable trip, not as much for what we accomplished each day, but for what the journey offered us in our life as a family.

In this process of discerning God's will and direction as believers and as a church, we, too, should remember:

The journey *IS* our destination.

First, we must acknowledge that we have been in a process of discerning God's will and direction in our lives and in our ministries for some time. In other words, many of us stepped in the stream a while ago, and yet we have all, at some time or another, stepped back out of the stream deciding to do things our own way. Throughout our lives, we step into, and back out of, the stream of God's will over and over again. Therefore, the best part of our journey is when we get into the stream of God's will and stay there by trusting God to take us where God desires us to go.

Second, we must resist the temptation in this process to make the accomplishment of tasks the end point which we seek. It is so easy to convince ourselves that if we can complete this process with a list of projects then we will be "successful." The model we are given for strategic planning in the U.S. corporate arena is to establish specific goals and tasks to accomplish each goal. The success of each year, and each person, therefore is assessed by whether or not these goals and tasks were accomplished.

> *When we step into the Stream of God's will, we relinquish control of the destination and how we'll get there.*

Although having goals and objectives is helpful for us in ministry, the history of God's people as told in Scripture suggests a very different model. "Success" among the people of God is defined not so much by the accomplishment of our humanly established goals but rather by our obedience to God's will and following the course God has set. Therefore, the most important task we have is to seek the will and direction that God has for us as defined by our mission and vision and then to live obediently into these.

Our journey, then, is to step into the stream of God's will so we can discern and claim God's purpose for us that will set the direction and course for our lives and ministry together. Once we claim that direction and course, then we must commit to staying in that stream and to assessing regularly any changes in the course that God is setting.

Plan Behind

According to the practices of the world, we are to plan strategically and carefully each step we take in carrying out the plans we have developed. Strategic planning is based on solid business practices of knowing where you need to go and developing specific steps to get there.

"Success" in our ministries should be defined by obedience to God's will.

God honors careful planning, and yet for our plans to honor God they must be consistent with God's will. James warns us about the risks of our planning apart from God when he says:

Look here, you people who say, "Today or tomorrow we are going to a certain town and will stay there a year. We will do business there and make a profit." How do you know what will happen tomorrow? For your life is like the morning fog—it's here a little while, then it's gone. What you ought to say is, "If the Lord wants us to, we will live and do this or that." Otherwise, you will be boasting about your own plans, and all such boasting is evil.
James 4:13-16 NLT

Planning is honorable, and even crucial, when we are acting in obedience to the will of God. However, apart from God, our plans can be arrogant, foolish, or even futile. Therefore, before we make any plans, we must create the sacred space and time to discern God's will by asking strategic questions and listening to God's guiding answers.

In Genesis 41, we hear the story of Joseph who was summoned from prison by Pharaoh to answer strategic questions. Joseph's interpretations of the Pharaoh's dreams revealed God's plan for Egypt. By listening to God's plan, Joseph was able to develop strategies and practical steps that would save a nation from famine. Joseph did so not by his own skill or knowledge alone but through the guidance of the Spirit of the Living God.

The world tells us to plan ahead. God's Word tells us to plan behind. Our biggest risk in planning for the future is getting too far ahead of God instead of staying behind the Cross and remaining firmly within God's will. To stay within God's will and to prevent getting ahead of God, we must make sure that we step in—and remain in—the stream.

Apart from adherence to God's will, our plans can be arrogant, foolish, and even futile.

Setting the Coordinates

As mentioned earlier, once we step into the stream of God's will, we submit ourselves to the direction and course that God has set for us as defined by our mission and vision. Another way to regard our mission and vision is the anchor which we cast before us to keep us firmly planted within God's will and to keep us from drifting off course. We place our confidence and hope, then, in God's purpose for us which will serve as a ***sure and steady anchor for our souls*. Hebrews 6:19**

George Barna, in his book *Turning Vision into Action*, describes our mission as the "grand purpose for which we exist." As

Christians, we have all been co-missioned to the same mission by Jesus when he said:

> *Therefore go and make disciples of all nations, baptizing them in the name of the Father and of the Son and of the Holy Spirit, and teaching them to obey everything I have commanded you. And surely I am with you always, to the very end of the age.*
>
> **Matthew 28:19-20 NIV**

Every church shares in the Great Commission that Jesus gave to all of us, and none of us can delegate this mission to another church or reject it as not being our own! Since all churches, then, share in the same mission, it is no surprise that our mission statements may sound very similar from church to church. The means by which each individual believer and church lives out this shared mission, however, are very different depending on our setting, circumstances, and calling.

Our God-given mission and vision is the Anchor which we cast.

What is unique and different in living out this shared co-mission is God's vision for us as individuals and as the church. Barna defines vision as "a clear and precise mental portrait of a preferable future, imparted by God to the chosen servants, based on an accurate understanding of God, self and circumstances." (*Turning Vision Into Action*, 36) God's vision for us will be unique and specific to who God has created us to be and what God has called us to do in bringing about the Kingdom here on earth. God's vision for us will be shaped by our unique call to ministry in the specific setting in which we find ourselves.

Once we are able to focus our vision, we will get incredible clarity in what God is calling us to do, and sometimes even greater clarity regarding what we are not being called to do. One of the most common downfalls in our ministries is that we are somehow convinced that we must do it all! God has not called us each to respond to all needs but rather to those needs which God has equipped and provided for us to meet. We will learn together to grab hold of the "best" in our ministry for the Kingdom and to let go of the "rest" in obedience to God's will for us.

The Journey as a Process

To be able to cast the anchor, defined by our mission and vision, we must enter into a process of serious discernment to make sure that we are casting the right anchor in the right place to keep us on God's right path for us. Therefore, stepping into God's will is a process to which we must commit together.

Together is a critical word in this formula. Throughout the history of God's people, God has consistently called us to move for God's sake while remaining in the context of community. God called Abram AND Sarai, Moses AND Aaron, Jesus AND the disciples, Paul AND Silas—to lead toward a community of faith to fulfill God's will among and through them.

We are called to fulfill God's will in the context of community.

Since God calls us in the context of community, it is also essential to acknowledge that there will be challenges and blessings as we learn to be and do together. As a community committed to living into God's will, we must go through a process of becoming and working as a group or team. Together, we must learn WHO we are, WHOSE we are, and WHAT it is God is calling us to do.

In the 1960's, educator Bruce Tuckman identified a general process that describes the life and work of groups together. This process of team development involves four phases: Forming, Storming, Norming, and Performing.

These four stages are sequential, cyclical, and actually essential to becoming a healthy and effective ministry team whether we represent church leadership, staff, or even a family.

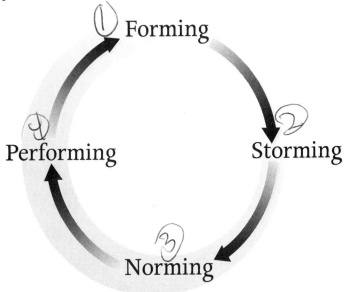

When we FORM as a group, we learn to BE with each other and how to relate to one another as individuals and as a team. Essential FORMING activities include gathering, greeting, getting to know God and each other and what we bring to the group. The focus of activity, therefore, in the FORMING phase is on our dwelling together—with God and one another—to foster the relationships among us.

In the FORMING phase, we cast the first anchor or our sea anchor which provides the boat stability and protection in the face of great turbulence and storms. As the early Christian church was forming, Paul was constantly reminding them WHO they were and WHOSE they were to anchor their life and ministry.

There is one body and one Spirit, just as you were called to the one hope of your calling, one Lord, one faith, one baptism, one God and Father of all, who is above all and through all and in all. But each of us was given grace according to the measure of Christ's gift. Therefore it is said, "When he ascended on high he made captivity itself a captive; he gave gifts to his people." (When it says, "He ascended," what does it mean but that he had also descended into the lower parts of the earth? He who descended is the same one who ascended far above all the heavens, so that he might fill all things.)

The gifts he gave were that some would be apostles, some prophets, some evangelists, some pastors and teachers, to equip the saints for the work of ministry, for building up the body of Christ, until all of us come to the unity of the faith and of the knowledge of the Son of God, to maturity, to the measure of the full stature of Christ.

We must no longer be children, tossed to and fro and blown about by every wind of doctrine, by people's trickery, by their craftiness in deceitful scheming. But speaking the truth in love, we must grow up in every way into him who is the head, into Christ, from whom the whole body, joined and knit together by every ligament with which it is equipped, as each part is working properly, promotes the body's growth in building itself up in love.

Ephesians 4:4-6, 11-16 NRSV

We, too, must remember WHO we are and WHOSE we are in

our calling in Jesus Christ. Furthermore, we must establish and enforce firm boundaries that will protect our relationships and ministries. Only then will we be able to withstand the turbulence and storms in our life and work together.

Because once we have Formed, we will STORM. STORMING is when we, as individuals, begin to articulate our views, opinions, wishes, needs and desires regarding our individual and corporate life and ministry. At times, our views, opinions, wishes, needs, or desires "strike together" causing conflict.

It is critical for us to remember that conflict is both natural and inevitable in any group, and storming is actually important for us to clarify WHAT it is God is calling us to do. Conflict, or STORMING, does not harm us as a group, but how we respond to the conflict can. What is essential in our moving through this process with integrity is knowing how to STORM in ways that strengthen our relationships with Jesus Christ and one another.

When we STORM, we refine and define WHAT we are about.

Frequently in our churches, we do not know how to STORM with integrity, so we either "avoid" the situation (which only allows the conflict to lie dormant until it erupts at a later time) or we leave. As a result, we often get stuck between FORMING and STORMING as we move back and forth between these two stages. The key, then, is to learn how to STORM together in ways that edify, and do not tear down, the individuals and the group.

Once we are able to STORM and answer the key questions regarding WHAT it is God is calling us to do, then we can NORM together as a team around our shared mission and vision. This is when we are able to cast the second anchor that guides and directs our course in the stream and keeps us from drifting off course, especially in the midst of subsequent storms.

In our NORMING together, we can say with assurance, "Yes, this IS what we are about!" as well as "No, that is NOT what we are about." Such clarity gives us freedom to move forward without being held back by the demands and expectations that are not from God. It is also important to remember that when we NORM, not everyone will agree with God's mission and vision for us, and some will even choose to part ways.

Each person is constantly faced with the choice of whether or not to continue on this journey guided by a particular mission and vision, and each of us must make this choice intentionally. There is honor in staying, and there is honor in leaving. Despite the grief and pain we may have in letting anyone go, we must learn to honor those who choose to leave because they can not agree on the group's mission and vision.

When the anchor is cast, clarifying who we are, whose we are, and what we are called to do, we can finally PERFORM the ministries that will bring bring about the Kingdom in our midst. In our PERFORMING, we are released to accomplish the GOD-things that will embody the mission and vision. Furthermore, by devoting the resources we have (people, time, money, facilities) to focus on doing the "God things," instead of doing lots of "good things," we can rest assured that there will always be sufficient resources to accomplish God's will.

> *When we PERFORM, we do the God-things by putting the vision into action.*

The "Ultimate Ministry Team"

Like any other group or team, Jesus and his disciples also journeyed through these four stages in their life and ministry. In the gospels, we hear about Jesus and the disciples first FORMING as they came together to define and refine WHO they were. In Luke, we hear the story of Jesus calling the first disciples:

> *When Simon Peter saw this happen, he knelt down in front of Jesus and said, "Lord, don't come near me! I am a sinner." Peter and everyone with him were completely surprised at all the fish they had caught. His partners James and John, the sons of Zebedee, were surprised too. Jesus told Simon, "Don't be afraid! From now on you will bring in people instead of fish."*
>
> **Luke 5:8-10** CEV

Throughout the gospel story, Jesus and the disciples dwelled with one another as they learned WHO they were, WHOSE they were and WHY they belonged together.

But in addition to Jesus and the disciples FORMING, we also hear about them STORMING. As their comfort and realness with one another increased, so did their willingness to share their differing views, opinions, wishes, needs, and desires. At the critical turning point on their journey where Jesus set his face to Jerusalem and the cross, Jesus also turned to his disciples and asked this pivotal question:

> *"Who do you say I am?" Simon Peter spoke up, "You are the Messiah, the Son of the living God." Jesus told him: "Simon, son of Jonah, you are blessed! You didn't discover this on your own. It was shown to you by my Father in heaven. So I will call you Peter, which means "a rock." On this rock I will build my church, and death itself will not have any power over it."*
>
> **Matthew 16:16-18** CEV

At this pivotal place on their journey, Jesus clarified WHO he was and WHO Peter was, and then he clarified the purpose for which he had been sent.

> *From then on, Jesus began telling his disciples what would happen to him. He said, "I must go to Jerusalem. There the nation's leaders, the chief priests, and the teachers of the Law of Moses will make me suffer terribly. I will be killed, but three days later I will rise to life." Peter took Jesus aside and told him to stop talking like that. He said, "God would never let this happen to you, Lord!" Jesus turned to Peter and said, "Satan, get away from me! You're in my way because you think like everyone else and not like God."*
>
> **Matthew 16:21-23** CEV

Jesus and Peter had differing views, opinions, wishes, needs and desires regarding WHO this Messiah was to be and what the Kingdom of God was to be about! Jesus and Peter were clearly STORMING.

Throughout their journey to the cross and beyond, Jesus and the disciples stormed in their seeking to understand their true vision and purpose for ministry together. Because of the paramount importance of their relationship and ministry, they persevered through the storming until they finally "got it." However, it wasn't until Pentecost when the Holy Spirit had been poured out on them that the disciples finally understood who Jesus was and what it meant to be co-laborers with him for the Kingdom of God.

Without healthy STORMING our NORMING will be shallow and useless.

After the Holy Spirit had descended on the day of Pentecost, Peter boldly cast the anchor when he said:

"So let it be clearly known by everyone in Israel that God has made this Jesus whom you crucified to be both Lord and Messiah!" Peter's words convicted them deeply, and they said to him and to the other apostles, "Brothers, what should we do?" Peter replied, "Each of you must turn from your sins and turn to God, and be baptized in the name of Jesus Christ for the forgiveness of your sins. Then you will receive the Holy Spirit…"
Those who believed what Peter said were baptized and added to the church—about three thousand in all. They joined with the other believers and devoted themselves to the apostles' teaching and fellowship sharing in the Lord's Supper and in prayer.

Acts 2:36-38, 41-42 NLT

Amazingly, once the disciples NORMED around WHO Jesus was and WHAT their ministry was to be about, they were able to PERFORM the God-things, the mighty wonders and acts of God that would bring about the Kingdom of God in their midst:

A deep sense of awe came over them all, and the apostles performed many miraculous signs and wonders. And all the believers met together constantly and shared everything they had. They sold their possessions and shared the proceeds with those in need. They worshiped together at the Temple each day, met in homes for the Lord's Supper, and shared their meals with great joy and generosity—all the while praising God and enjoying the goodwill of all the people. And each day the Lord added to their group those who were being saved.

Acts 2:43-47 NLT

We are called to be co-laborers in the Kingdom by performing the mighty works and wonders of God. God is calling us to let go of doing lots of good things and to channel the resources provided to do the God-things. This was not simply a phenomenon limited to the early church. This is God's promise for our church today! But before we can PERFORM the mighty wonders and works of God, we must first NORM around God's purpose and vision for us to bring about the Kingdom *on earth as it is in heaven.* And before we can NORM, we must be able and willing to STORM in ways that strengthen our relationships with Jesus Christ and one another. Lastly (and first!), before we can STORM we must come together and FORM as we learn WHO we are and WHOSE we are on this journey of faith.

When Will We Get There?

In a world driven by destinations and acclimated to accomplishments, we struggle with the concept that our ministry is less about completed tasks and more about our obedience to God's will. One crucial thing for us to remember as we embark on this journey of discerning and living into God's will is that we may not reach the "final destination" on this side of eternity. In other words, our "tasks" will never be completed until the final "race" is finished. However, we are called to run that race with endurance and fervor since the race, or the journey, is the destination.

Performing the mighty works of God was not limited to the early church.

> *Therefore, since we are surrounded by such a huge crowd of witnesses to the life of faith, let us strip off every weight that slows us down, especially the sin that hinders our progress. And let us run with endurance the race that God has set before us. We do this by keeping our eyes on Jesus, on whom our faith depends from start to finish.*
> **Hebrews 12:1-2 NLT**

The Kingdom of God is our ultimate destination, and yet the JOURNEY itself is what we hope to complete. The journey did not begin with us, and it will not end with us. Instead, we step into the stream of God's will along with a long procession of faithful sojourners who are contending together for the Kingdom of God. Our focus, therefore, is not implementing what's on our minds, but rather on discerning the mind of God.

Trust in the Lord with all your heart;

do not depend on your own understanding.

Seek his will in all you do,

And he will direct your paths.

Proverbs 3:5-6

Questions for Discussion

1. How can doing lots of "good things" keep us from doing the "God-things" God is calling us to accomplish.

2. When have we experienced or seen the Kingdom of God made manifest around us?

3. Share with others a trip you have taken when the journey itself was more important than the destination.

4. When have our own plans interfered with God's will?

5. How are we living out the Great Commission as stated in Matthew 28:19-20? How does our mission statement embody the Great Commission?

The Right Next Step for Chapter Two

Schedule a time for a fellowship meal together. During the meal share with one another significant aspects of your own faith journey. End your time together with worship and Communion.

Scripture & Prayers

The following prayers are written to be prayed as individual prayers and as prayers for the church. You may substitute the words "my church" in place of the word "me" or "I" to make the prayer one for your church. Pray them at home and pray them together during your study sessions.

Focus Notes

Day 1
Genesis 16:7-8
The angel of the Lord found Hagar near a spring in the desert; it is the spring that is beside the road to Shinar. And he said, "Hagar, servant of Sarai, where are you coming from and where are you going?" NIV

Lord God, thank you for finding me before I find you; thank you for looking for me when I am looking for direction but fail to look to you. Help me to remember that you are the spring in the desert, and the stream from that spring never runs dry. Teach me to step into the stream, because it always leads to you. All other roads lead to the desert.

Day 2
Jeremiah 42:1-3
Then all the army officers…and all the people from the least to
the greatest approached Jeremiah the prophet and said to him,
"Please hear our petition and pray to the Lord your God for this
entire remnant. For as you now see, though we were once many,
now only a few are left. Pray that the Lord your God will tell us
where we should go and what we should do." NIV
Proverbs 20:24
All our steps are ordered by the Lord. How then can we understand our own ways? NRSV

Lord, only you know where I
am to go and what I am to do.
I cannot see it for myself nor
understand it from where I sit.
Help me to listen to your voice
of direction. Silence the voice of
my flesh and the voices around
me. Help me to trust you with
my whole heart. Help me to do
the things of God.

Focus Notes

Day 3
Genesis 11:1-4
Now the whole world had
one language and a common
speech. As men moved east-
ward they found a plain in Shinar and settled there. They said to
each other, "Come let's make bricks and bake them thoroughly."
They used brick instead of stone and tar for mortar. Then they
said, "Come let us build ourselves a city, with a tower that reaches
to the heavens, so that we can make a name for ourselves and not
be scattered over the face of the whole earth." NIV

Jeremiah 10:23
I know, O Lord, that the way of human beings is not in their control, that mortals as they walk cannot direct their steps. NRSV

O God, you have made us to be a people of movement. Help me neither to settle nor to think I have arrived. Help me to stay in the stream of your will and not stay tied to the shore. Help me to remember that your streams never stop. Let me not become stagnant in a sea of self-focused activity. Keep me looking at you. Direct me to build your kingdom and not my own. I have been bought with price, and my life is not my own. Your Kingdom come, your will be done.

Focus Notes

Day 4
Philippians 3:12
Not that I have already obtained all this, or have already been made perfect, but I press on to take hold of that which Christ Jesus took hold of me. NIV

Jesus, I will never arrive. I will never finish. I will never succeed until I see your face. Help me to press on and to persevere in the daily ebb and flow of time and pressure. Remind me that the journey is the destination, and that I am also to bear a cross on this journey. Thank you for bearing it for me, before me, and with me. Help me to take hold of you as you have taken hold of me and called me your own. You will set my course and my direction.

Day 5
Proverbs 16:9
We can make our plans, but the Lord determines our steps. NLT

Lord, help me to plan according to your will and not my own. Teach me how to listen and how to discern your voice from my own and other's. Give me an undivided heart to know you and one that rightly divides the Truth. Correct my steps and correct my course, Jesus. You are the Chief Shepherd. Lead me in paths of righteousness for your name's sake.

Focus Notes

Day 6
Galatians 1:15b-16
For it pleased God in his kindness to choose me and call me, even before I was born! What undeserved mercy! Then he revealed his Son to me so that I could proclaim the Good News about Jesus to the Gentiles. When all this happened to me, I did not rush out to consult with anyone else. NLT

God, you have a specific purpose for me just as you had for Paul. You have set me apart from birth to accomplish it. Help me focus my vision on you and your will for me. Help me to let go of that to which I am not called. Help me to remember that I am fearfully and wonderfully made for your purposes. Help me to rejoice in who you have called and created me uniquely to be. You are the author and finisher of my faith and my ministry.

Day 7
2 Timothy 4:7-8
I have fought the good fight, I have finished the race, and I have kept the faith. Now there is in store for me the crown of righteousness, which the Lord, the righteous Judge, will award to me that day—and not only to me, but also to those who longed for his appearing. NIV

Let it be so, Lord Jesus. May I be able to finish the race set before me with endurance. My reward is in Heaven. My reward is you. It is to finally see your face. Help me to remember that the journey is a road of relationship with you. If I close my eyes to what you have placed around me or only focus on the end point, I miss you. The journey is the destination. And that destination is you, Jesus.

Trust in the Lord
with all your heart;
do not depend
on your own
understanding.
Seek his will
in all you do,
And he will direct
your paths.

Proverbs 3:5-6

Two

Reclaiming the Rhythm of God

So often when we are called together as a group, we expect to get right to work. After all, there is often too much to do with too little time and resources to do it. Therefore, we want to say, "Forget this forming, storming, and norming stuff. Let's get to the performing and move on!" We live in a fast-paced world that never stops where our lives and churches are driven by the demands to accomplish and acquire more and more. In contrast, all of life demonstrates that there is a limit to our doing when there is no time or space for being.

Today, the world tries to convince us that rest and stillness are signs of weakness. In response to this pressure, we set ourselves up for disaster in our refusal to dwell. In fact, most human-made disasters, such as the sinking of the *Titanic* or the *Exxon Valdez* oil spill, occur in the wee hours of the morning when our created rhythm says "rest." However, in our arrogant drive to get ahead, we insist on doing to the point we cease to be.

God created all of life to live and thrive based on God-established rhythms such as the annual, seasonal and lunar cycles, the ebb and flow of tides, the rising and setting of the sun. These naturally established rhythms of life are fundamental and essential to both plants and animals. We as humans are no exception.

The human body itself relies on an intricate array of rhythms from the beating of our hearts to the flow of hormones. Much of the disease and dysfunction within our bodies can be traced to disruption of these created rhythms.

Breathing In–Breathing Out

Of all the established rhythms of life, breathing in and breathing out is one of the most essential to our surviving and thriving as humans. Every moment of every day, we are completely dependent on this subconscious rhythm without which we could not live. In fact, any disruption in this rhythm is quickly noticed by the body with compensatory mechanisms kicking in. We must breathe in, and then we must breathe out. One is not sufficient without the other.

Another way to understand this rhythm of life is in our rhythm of being and doing. When we breathe in, we "be." When we breathe out, we "do." From the beginning of time, God established this essential rhythm of being and doing—of resting and working, of dormancy and producing. However, in our arrogance and drive, we have often adopted a dysrhythmia of doing, doing, doing—of breathing out, breathing out, breathing out. As a result, we find ourselves worn-out and breathless and unable to remember who we "be."

Our lives are based on the rhythm of breathing in and breathing out–of being and doing.

In Exodus, God commanded us to adhere to this rhythm of being and doing through our honoring of Sabbath:

Tell the people of Israel to keep my Sabbath day for the Sabbath is a sign of the covenant between me and you forever. It helps you to remember that I am the LORD who makes you holy. Anyone who desecrates it must die; anyone who works on that day will be cut off from the community. Work six days only, but the seventh day must be a day of total rest… For in six days the LORD made heaven and earth, but he rested on the seventh day and was refreshed.

Exodus 31:13-17 NLT

God established the weekly rhythm of work and Sabbath rest, a rhythm that must be honored so we can remember that God is God—and we are not! When we refuse to be still and know that God is God, our performing quickly becomes all about us and what we can do and rapidly falls short of the wonders of God. Therefore, to "be" about performing the mighty wonders of God, we must intentionally set aside the sacred time and space to "be" with God.

In addition to the weekly rhythm of Sabbath, we must also embrace a daily rhythm of "being" with God and "doing" for God. How can we know how to serve the Lord if we do not take time to know the Lord we serve?

> *Now as they went on their way, he entered a certain village, where a woman named Martha welcomed him into her home. She had a sister named Mary, who sat at the Lord's feet and listened to what he was saying. But Martha was distracted by her many tasks; so she came to him and asked, "Lord, do you not care that my sister has left me to do all the work by myself? Tell her then to help me." But the Lord answered her, "Martha, Martha, you are worried and distracted by many things; there is need of only one thing. Mary has chosen the better part, which will not be taken away from her."*

Luke 10:38-42 NRSV

Mary was embracing the Sabbath moments within a day, setting aside her "doing" for the Lord to "be" with her Lord. Like Mary, we too must daily set aside our "doing" to create the sacred time and space to be with God. For it is there, in those Sabbath moments of being with God in solitude, prayer, and seeking the Scriptures, where we come to know who God really is and who God is calling us to be. Before we can breathe out, we must breathe in. Before we can "do," we must be able to "be."

Remembering WHO We Are and WHOSE We Are

Our function, or what we do, must flow from our identity, or the core sense of WHO we are and WHOSE we are. Jesus described this dynamic of identity and function when he said to his disciples:

> *Yes, I am the vine; you are the branches. Those who remain in me, and I in them, will produce much fruit. For apart from me you can do nothing.*
>
> **John 15:5** NLT

Jesus states that we must "be" in relationship with him and with one another before we can produce any fruit, or "do" anything for the sake of God, the Gardener. Apart from this relationship, we can do nothing at all that matters for the sake of the Kingdom of God. In other words, we can do lots of "good things," but we can't do the "God-things" without dwelling with and remaining with God and one another as believers.

> **Remain in me, and I will remain in you.**
> **For a branch cannot produce fruit if it is severed from the**
> **vine, and you cannot be fruitful apart from me.**
>
> **John 15:4** NLT

Furthermore, we cannot actively engage in works for any extended period of time that are inconsistent with the character and nature of who we are. Neil T. Anderson, in his book *Victory Over the Darkness* describes the importance of our identity being grounded in Jesus Christ when he says, "People cannot consistently behave in ways that are inconsistent with the way they perceive themselves" (47)

47

What we do in our life and ministries will be determined by WHO we are and WHOSE we are and the character and nature of those relationships that define us. In other words, if we are rooted firmly in healthy relationships with Jesus Christ and one another, then we will be able to produce godly fruit that reflects the character and nature of these relationships. However, if we do not dedicate the sacred time and space to nurture healthy relationships with Jesus Christ and one another, then our fruit will reflect the dis-ease that is there.

> *Likewise every good tree bears good fruit, but a bad tree bears bad fruit. A good tree cannot bear bad fruit, and a bad tree cannot bear good fruit. Every tree that does not bear good fruit is cut down and thrown into the fire. Thus, by their fruit you will recognize them.*
>
> **Matthew 7:17-20** NIV

Healthy relationships, however, do not just happen. They must be cultivated in an environment that allows us to "be" together—to breathe in with one another—without the constant pressures of doing and performing. We must be able to come together and FORM as a group in ways that remind us WHO we are and WHOSE we are so our sea anchor can be cast. With that first anchor, the sea anchor, deployed, we can safely withstand great turbulence and storms. However, without this sea anchor in place, in the midst of the storms, we get tossed back and forth from one opinion to another, and we are at risk of our ministries drifting way off course.

Healthy relationships produce healthy ministries.

Diseased relationships will produce diseased ministries.

Momma's Kitchen Table

Growing up in a small mill town in the South, my family began and ended every day around my momma's kitchen table. The table was made of knotty pine which my daddy had crafted out of an old pew from my momma's childhood church. It was there, at the kitchen table, during breakfast and supper that we shared stories of our life together. We shared our blessings and our burdens, our triumphs and trials. It was there at the table where my brothers and I were reminded WHO we were and WHOSE we were as we came and went in our doing.

Dr. Rachel Naomi Remen, in her book *Kitchen Table Wisdom*, describes the importance of this sacred time and space to dwell with another:

"**Everybody is a story. When I was a child, people sat around the kitchen tables and told their stories. We don't do that much anymore. Setting around the table telling stories is not just a way of passing time. It is the way the wisdom gets passed along. The stuff that helps us to live a life worth remembering... Real stories take time. We stopped telling stories when we started to lose that sort of time, pausing time, reflecting time, wondering time. Life rushes us along and few people are strong enough to stop on their own....**

All relationships require the sacred time and space to be nurtured and fed.

Most parents know that importance of telling children their own story, over and over again, so that they come to know in the tellings who they are and to whom they belong. At the kitchen table we do this for each other." (xxvii)

Sociologists have noted that the unraveling of society can in some ways be traced to the disappearance of the kitchen table. These days, we find fewer and fewer families are gathered at the table for the sharing of meals and stories. Without this set-apartness of sacred time and space, our rootedness is lost. Without a clear sense of identity, our function becomes blurred. Without a healthy sense of WHO we are and WHOSE we are, what we do can get way off track.

Coming Together

The solution obviously is not simply reclaiming the kitchen table but rather reclaiming those sacred spaces and times where we come together to share our stories and The Story that reminds us who we are called to be as the people of God. The power of the kitchen table is that it represents the time and space that is set apart where we come together, break bread, share stories, and dwell.

Without a clear sense of identity, our function becomes blurred.

In the book of Acts, the word often used for "church" is the Greek work *ekklesia* which refers to an assembly or gathering of God's people. To do the work of God, we must first come together as the people of God. We hear in Acts that the early church came together as often as they could to root themselves in this new identity in Christ and in their new experience as a Christian community. Alone, they would never be able to withstand the storms of persecution, and yet by coming together, they were nurtured in God's Word and by one another.

> *And all the believers met together constantly and shared everything they had. They sold their possessions and shared the proceeds with those in need. They worshiped together at the Temple each day, met in homes for the Lord's Supper, and shared their meals with great joy and generosity—all the while praising God and enjoying the goodwill of all the*

people. And each day the Lord added to their group those who were being saved.

Acts 2:44-47 NLT

The early Christians came together constantly sharing all they had—including their meals. Like the early believers, it's often the food that draws us together. Throughout the Gospels, we hear that Jesus, too, often nurtured the relationships around a meal. Jesus feasted with sinners, fellowshiped with Pharisees, and lingered with Lazarus, Mary, and Martha. It was even around a meal, at the Last Supper, where Jesus reminded the disciples WHO they were and WHOSE they were and the purpose for which they were called. And after the Resurrection, it was in the breaking of the bread and in a shared meal when their eyes were opened and they recognized the Savior in their midst.

Breaking bread together is central to our FORMING in ministry.

In chapter one of Acts, we hear that for forty days after the Resurrection, the believers gathered around the table, and time and time again, Jesus showed up. We can only imagine the conversations they had around that table. They probably wept and asked forgiveness for their desertion and denial. But as they broke the bread, undoubtedly the hurts of the past melted away, and their hope for the future was restored as Jesus continued to share his vision of the Kingdom yet to come.

As it was for Jesus and his disciples, it is for us when we gather and break bread together both as a shared meal and sharing in the Lord's Supper. Both our bodies and our relationships are strengthened and nourished. Around the table and through the meal that is shared, the animosities of the past can fade away, and the hope for our future can start to take shape. Failures can be forgotten and forgiveness given. Stories of the past are told, and the dreams for the future shared.

Engaging in Holy Conversation

The food may bring us to the table, but it's the conversation that will keep us there. Long after the food is gone, the conversation continues on when we set apart the time and space to do so. And our conversation is transformed into holy conversation when we invite God to be an active participant. When our stories are woven in the context of The Story, when in that sacred space and time we share how God is working in us and among us, our conversations, too, become sacred and set apart.

> *We must dwell with God and one another to hear how our stories form*

Hidden in all stories is the One Story. The more we listen, the clearer the Story becomes. Our true identity, who we are, why we are here, what sustains us, is in this story. *(Kitchen Table Wisdom, xxix)*

But how do we invite God to become an active participant in our conversations? God actively informs and transforms our conversations when we actively seek the holy voice in our midst. God becomes an active participant when we ask one another, "How did you see God at work in your life this week?" and truly expect that we did. God's voice is invited into the conversation when we ask, "What does scripture tell us about this?" or "How does God's Word inform you in this matter?"

When we set apart the sacred time and space to FORM together, our lives and stories are woven together with the life and story of our Savior, Jesus Christ. In the weaving of our stories in

Christ, we learn WHO we are and WHOSE we are in a way that binds us to Jesus Christ and one another. However, without Jesus at the center of our coming together, our relationships can easily unravel when tension is placed on any part of the relationship. And yet, with Jesus as the central strand of our cord, we are woven together in a way that not only withstands but is strengthened in the midst of tension and strife.

When we FORM as a group by coming and dwelling together with Jesus Christ as the central focus, we can resolutely deploy our first anchor to withstand any storm. There, we reclaim the rhythm of God—of breathing in so we can effectively breathe out. There we learn to "be" the people of God before we go forth to "do" the work of God.

Questions for Discussion

1. How do we observe Sabbath on a weekly basis as individuals? As families? As a church or ministry?

2. How do we intentionally dwell with God and one another on a daily basis?

3. In what ways are we, or our ministries, worn out and breathless?

4. How have we seen the health (or dis-ease) of our relationships affect our ministries?

The Right Next Step for Chapter Three

Assign individuals in your group to prepare a timeline which depicts the history of your ministry or church. Include on the timeline significant dates and events that indicate how, when and where God has acted in your midst.

At your next gathering, review this timeline together adding and editing as necessary. Additionally, each person present should share how and when they chose to become a part of this unfolding story.

Take special note of recurring patterns or circumstances which might indicate how God has been (and still is!) working through your history.

Note: A timeline is available for download in various formats at www.steppinginthestream.org.

Scriptures & Prayers

Day 1

Genesis 2:2-3

And on the seventh day God finished the work that he had done, and he rested on the seventh day from all the work that he had done.

So God blessed the seventh day and hallowed it, because on it God rested from all the work that he had done in creation. NRSV

Mark 2: 27

Then Jesus said to them, "The Sabbath was made to benefit people, and not people to benefit the Sabbath." NLT

Lord, from the foundation of the world you established a time for rest. You, the Creator, rested from your work. You blessed it and called it "holy." Lord, help us see that this is your call to us out of Eden. You are calling us back from toil to rest. Teach us to honor your call to "rest" and, in doing so, to honor you. Bring us back from the curse of the soil to the Garden of Rest.

> **Focus Notes**

Day 2

Genesis 2:7

The Lord God formed the man from the dust of the ground and breathed into his nostrils and the breath of life, and the man became a living being. NIV

Gracious God, you created us to "be." Your breath gave us life, and you created us in your image. Help us to be mindful of that Breath within us. In order to do your mighty works, we must first "be." Remind us that we must breathe in and become renewed and refilled with your Spirit, or we will die.

Day 3
Ezekiel 20:12
Keep my Sabbaths holy, that they may be a sign between us. Then you will know that I am the Lord your God. NIV

Focus Notes

Lord God, help us remember that you are God, and you are Lord. Help us to understand and real-ize that you alone are holy. Let us set ourselves apart and set a day apart that is holy. You have called us to be a people set apart. Help us to honor that calling by being a people of Sabbath. Let that not only be a sign between us but also a sign to the world.

Day 4
Psalm 46:10
Be still, and know that I am God. NIV
1 Kings 19:12
And after the earthquake there was a fire, but the LORD was not

in the fire. And after the fire there was the sound of a gentle whisper. NLT

Lord God, help us to let things be and to be still. Help us to trust that we can let go and know that you are still working. Remind us that before we can "do" we must "be." We must "be still" so we can "know." You are found in the quiet and the calm. You are a God of peace and not chaos. We cannot see you nor hear you until we are still. Help us to be still so we can hear your gentle whisper and know you are talking to us as Elijah heard you in that cave.

Focus Notes

Day 5
Numbers 9: 15-18
On the day the tabernacle was set up, the cloud covered the tabernacle, the tent of the covenant; and from evening until morning it was over the tabernacle, having the appearance of fire. It was always so: the cloud covered it by day and the appearance of fire by night. Whenever the cloud lifted from over the tent, then the Israelites would set out; and in the place where the cloud settled down, there the Israelites would camp. At the command of the Lord the Israelites would set out, and at the command of the Lord they would camp. As long as the cloud rested over the tabernacle, they would remain in camp. NRSV

Lord, you move us and you settle us. You settle us and leave us camped in our community. Teach us to build and nurture our relationships during these times. Remind us that we must come together and form as a group and a community before we can perform your works. Help us to acknowledge times of stillness as times of relationship. Teach us how to build and how to grow with one another while your cloud is still. Prevent us from moving ahead of you and prevent us from moving if we are not unified.

Day 6
Luke 10:38-42

Focus Notes

Jesus came to a village where a woman opened her home to him. She had a sister called Mary who sat at the Lord's feet listening to what he said. But Martha was distracted by all the preparations that had to be made.... "Martha, Martha," the Lord answered, "You are worried about many things, but only one thing is needed. Mary has chosen what is better, and it will not be taken away from her." NIV

Jesus, Mary sought that which could not be taken from her. She sought to know you. She knew WHO she was and WHOSE she was. Teach us how to sit at your feet, Jesus. We want to be like Mary and desire only you. We want to know the One who first loved us. When we can rest at your feet, then we will be able to stand and endure our struggles as a people and as a church. Help us all come together at your feet, Lord. Let not one of us be busy

58

with that which is unnecessary.

Day 7
John 21: 9-10,12
When they landed they saw a fire of burning coals there with fish on it and some bread. Jesus said to them, "Bring some of the fish you have just caught…. Come have breakfast." NIV

Lord, just as you so many times brought your disciples together over a meal, so you bring us. You bring us together to a common meal to remind us that we are all a common people. Help us to honor these times as sacred times, and remember you are there with us. Help us to remember that this is just a dim reflection of what you are preparing for us in heaven. As we come together at the table with our differing needs and desires, remind us that one day we will all be at the one table in Heaven. Let us not forget that as you and God are one, you have called us to be one. Unify us at your table, and prepare us for the Great Wedding Feast.

Trust in the Lord
with all your heart;
do not depend
on your own
understanding.
Seek his will
in all you do,
And he will direct
your paths.
Proverbs 3:5-6

Three

Weaving Our Stories with The Story

*W*hen we come together as a group to fulfill God's will among us, we commit ourselves and our resources to bringing about the Kingdom of God in our midst. In this context, we also understand that our work will not be completed until the final "race" is finished. Again, we must remember: The journey is our destination, and obedience to God's will, or staying in the stream, is our goal. Therefore, our journey of faith happens one right next step at a time.

God Calling
To Be
to Do

Therefore, the focus of this process is to discern God's will and direction for us in our lives and in our ministries. We are discerning WHO God is calling us to BE and WHAT God is calling us to DO as we bring about the Kingdom here on earth.

Fulfilling the will of God is a long journey. In fact, it is a life-long journey marked by many twists and turns, openings and closings, opportunities and obstacles. Every journey tells a story, and the stories told reveal the true nature of the journey. Through our stories, we learn WHO we are and WHOSE we are and how we got to WHERE we are today. In the sacred space and time of dwelling together, we can hear how our stories are woven together with THE Story, and we hear how our history impacts our future.

How Our Past Shapes Our Future

Every individual and every church has a history—a story to be told that explains who we are and where we are today. As any historian will attest, knowing our history is essential to understanding our present and preparing us for our future. Our history undoubtedly informs us of our past and in part forms our present. However, we must remember that it is the work of the Holy Spirit that transforms us for what God has in store for our future.

There is a clear distinction between letting our past inform us and wanting to stay there! Our past can be very alluring, and sometimes in the re-telling of our history, we start to long for the "glory" days. It's amazing how the passage of time can blur the memories of the past. The Israelites were only days out of bondage when they started longing for the things left behind and cried out to Moses:

> *Why did you ever take us out of Egypt?*
> *Why did you bring us here?*
>
> **Exodus 17:3** NLT

How soon we forget! When faced with struggles in the present or uncertainties of our future, it's sometimes easy to long for the ways things were. At other times, remembering the past can be very painful, so we avoid the re-telling of the stories. However, without the telling of our history, we run the risk of repeating mistakes, failing commitments, and missing out on the promises to be fulfilled.

Our history informs, but God's grace transforms.

We live in the tension between what we have been and what God yet desires us to be. Once we remember the past through the telling of our stories, we can let go of anything that is holding us back to grab hold of God's promising future ahead. There is a time to remember and a time to forget. Paul described this tension when he said:

> *I don't mean to say that I have already achieved these things or that I have already reached perfection! But I keep work-*

ing toward that day when I will finally be all that Christ Jesus saved me for and wants me to be. No, dear brothers and sisters, I am still not all I should be, but I am focusing all my energies on this one thing. Forgetting the past and looking forward to what lies ahead, I strain to reach the end of the race and receive the prize for which God, through Christ Jesus, is calling us up to heaven.

Philippians 3:12-14 NLT

Paul may very well have wanted to forget the past in which he participated in the imprisonment and destruction of believers. However, it was important to know Paul's past to see how the Holy Spirit transformed him for the future. So it is with us. We may all have situations or occurrences in our past—as individuals and as congregations—which we would rather forget due to our failings in mind, body, or spirit. However, there is healing and power in telling the past, in giving witness to how we are different today, and in articulating hope for tomorrow. Our history informs us, but God's grace, through the sanctifying and perfecting work of the Spirit, transforms us to become all God wants us, and saved us, to be. Only then will we experience the true glory days—the day when we will bring glory to God.

Function Flows from Identity

Understanding our history also helps us to see that what we do stems from who we are. The book of Deuteronomy is a beautiful example of how knowing our past empowers us to claim our future. As the Israelites stood on the border to the Promised Land, their leader, Moses paused to prepare them for what lay ahead. To prepare them for the future, Moses reviewed their past. He wanted them to know clearly WHO they were, WHOSE they were, and how they got to WHERE they were on their journey.

Over a period of weeks, Moses reminded the Israelites first of who God was as the living, loving, and sovereign God and who they were as a chosen but rebellious people. In reviewing their history, Moses wanted them to see that their function (what they did) flowed from their identity (who they were). First, Moses reminded them that God was a saving God who liberated them from slavery in Egypt, and a loving God who established a covenant with them to protect their relationship, and a gracious God who set before them a land flowing with milk and honey. In telling their stories, Moses also revealed that as a chosen people, they were called out and set apart by God, not because of what they had done, but because of who God was.

Every history tells a story of WHO *we are,* WHOSE *we are, and How we got* WHERE *we are.*

> *For you are a holy people, who belong to the LORD your God. Of all the people on earth, the LORD your God has chosen you to be his own special treasure.*

> *The LORD did not choose you and lavish his love on you because you were larger or greater than the other nations, for you were the smallest of all the nations! It was simply because the LORD loves you, and because he was keeping the oath he had sworn to your ancestors. That is why the LORD rescued you with such amazing power from your slavery under Pharaoh in Egypt. Understand, therefore, that the LORD your God is indeed God.*
>
> **Deuteronomy 7:6-9** NLT

Moses also reminded them that as a rebellious people, they repeatedly threatened the integrity of the covenant God had established:

> *When I looked, I saw that you had sinned against the LORD your God; you had made for yourselves an idol cast in the*

*shape of a calf. You had turned aside quickly from the way
that the LORD had commanded you.*

*You have been rebellious against the LORD ever since I have
known you. I lay prostrate before the LORD those forty days
and forty nights because the LORD had said he would destroy
you.*

Deuteronomy 9:16, 24-25 NIV

In reviewing the history of the past forty years, Moses
emphasized that it wasn't the geographical distance they had to
overcome to enter into the Promised Land. Instead, their past
demonstrated that it was the condition of their hearts which
created the greatest distance between them and God's promising
future.

Moses, like Paul, knew the value in reviewing the past, but he
also called them to move boldly forward into their future.

*This very day the Lord your God is commanding you to
observe these statutes and ordinances; so observe them diligently with all your heart and with all your soul. Today you
have obtained the Lord's agreement: to be your God; and for
you to walk in his ways, to keep his statutes, his commandments, and his ordinances, and to obey him. Today the Lord
has obtained your agreement: to be his treasured people, as he
promised you, and to keep his commandments; for him to set
you high above all nations that he has made, in praise and in
fame and in honor; and for you to be a people holy to the Lord
your God, as he promised.*

Deuteronomy 26:16-19 NRSV

Out of their past, Moses led the Israelites to claim their future
with a renewed understanding of WHO they were, WHOSE they
were, and WHAT God was calling them to BE and to DO. Their
history had informed them, but God's grace would transform

them to be a holy nation for the purpose of bringing praise, honor, and glory to God.

Procession of Faith

The history of God's people consists of stories of faith, and each of our personal stories is a part of that history. Scripture is filled with the stories of God's people and their journey to faithfulness.

> *By faith,*
> *we step in—and stay*
> *in—the stream.*

And yet the real power of Scripture is that their stories represent our stories. In reading God's Word, we can hear our own triumphs and falls in faith as we read the stories of the people stepping into—and back out of—God's will.

The book of Hebrews was written to encourage Jewish Christians to stay in the stream of God's will by believing and trusting in Jesus Christ. According to Hebrews, the key to getting in and staying in the stream is faith.

> *What is faith? It is the confident assurance that what we hope for is going to happen. It is the evidence of things we cannot yet see. God gave his approval to people in days of old because of their faith.*

Hebrews 11:1-2 NLT

Chapter eleven of Hebrews tells the stories of God's people who, by faith, moved through the struggles of the past to claim God's promise for the future. From the creation of the universe, God's people have processed forward in faith trusting that the promise God has set before them will, in fact, come to pass.

> *By faith Abraham, when called to go to a place he would later receive as his inheritance, obeyed and went, even though he did not know where he was going. By faith he made his home in the promised land like a stranger in a foreign country; he*

lived in tents, as did Isaac and Jacob, who were heirs with him of the same promise. For he was looking forward to the city with foundations, whose architect and builder is God.
Hebrews 11:8-10 NIV

Abraham chose to step into God's will because he trusted and knew who God was, not because he trusted and knew the place or the circumstances to which God was calling him. And Abraham remained in the stream of God's will not because God's promise for him had been fulfilled, but because he believed that God had a bigger and broader plan that extended way beyond him. In fact, Hebrews tells us that none of those faithful sojourners saw God's full promise come to fruition. Their commitment was not based on getting what they thought they deserved for stepping in. Instead, they got in the stream and stayed there because of their faith in who God was and what God would do for the fulfillment of a grander purpose beyond themselves.

> *We must be motivated by a purpose beyond ourselves.*

> *Every one of those people died. But they still had faith, even though they had not received what they had been promised. They were glad just to see these things from far away, and they agreed that they were only strangers and foreigners on this earth. When people talk this way, it is clear that they are looking for a place to call their own. If they had been talking about the land where they had once lived, they could have gone back at any time. But they were looking forward to a better home in heaven. That's why God wasn't ashamed for them to call him their God. He even built a city for them.*
> **Hebrews 11:13-16** CEV

Hebrews reminds us that it is by faith that we step in and remain the stream of God's will—not for what we desire to obtain, but for the fulfillment of God's plan. In doing so, we trust that God's plan is not only what is right and good for God, but that we will know *how good and pleasing and perfect his will really is* for us as well (Romans 12:2).

Fulfilling the will of God is a journey of faith that begins with trusting who God is instead of what we can do. It is by faith in WHO God is that we step into the stream of God's will. It is by faith in WHAT God will do in us, through us, and among us that we choose to stay there.

From Observation to Obedience

Many voices and forces will try to convince us that the cost and risk of stepping in are too great when we are not "assured" of immediate return. When we commit our lives and our ministries to doing the "God things" and not just the "good things," we can be sure that there will be significant cost and risk involved. When Jesus called his disciples and others to follow him, he knew clearly that there would be risk involved and costly sacrifices to make. And yet Jesus did not hesitate to require complete loyalty to the calling, regardless of the cost.

> *Stepping in the stream requires letting go of our own desires.*

Then he called his disciples and the crowds to come over and listen. "If any of you wants to be my follower," he told them, "you must put aside your selfish ambitions, shoulder your cross, and follow me. If you try to keep your life for yourself, you will lose it. But if you give up your life for my sake and for the sake of the Good News, you will find true life."

Mark 9:34-35 NLT

Jesus extended the invitation and call to all of us to be his followers and to participate in bringing about the Kingdom of God in our midst. However, Jesus clearly told us that the cost of stepping in requires a willingness to let go of our own ambitions and desires so we can "shoulder the cross" by submitting ourselves completely to God's will.

Dietrich Bonhoeffer, in his book *The Cost of Discipleship*, refers to this step as "single-minded obedience."

When he was challenged by Jesus to accept a life of voluntary poverty, the rich young man knew he was faced with the simple alternative of obedience or disobedience. When Levi was called from the receipt of custom and Peter from his nets, there was no doubt that Jesus meant business. Both of them were to leave everything and follow. Again, when Peter was called to walk on the rolling sea, he had to get up and risk his life. Only one thing was required in each case—to rely on Christ's word, and cling to it as offering greater security than all the securities in the world. The forces which tried to interpose themselves between the word of Jesus and the response of obedience were as formidable then as they are today... But the call of Jesus made short work of all these barriers and created obedience. That call was the Word of God himself, and all that it required was single-minded obedience. (87)

When the call is compelling the cost is inconsequential!

All of us are called to step into the stream, but we each have to choose if and when we do so, as individuals and as a church. In faith, there comes a time when the call of Jesus Christ, as heard through the means of grace, is so compelling that the cost becomes inconsequential. There comes a point on our journey of faith when we realize that the cost of disobedience is much greater then the cost of obedience. That is the point at which we move from standing on the bank in observation to stepping into the stream in obedience.

From THEY to WE

There is a remarkable difference between telling someone else's story and claiming it as your own. At times, we find some safety in distance when describing a faith journey. Luke is known as one of the greatest historians in the New Testament for his descriptions of the life and ministry of Jesus (in the Gospel of Luke) and of the early church (in the book of Acts). Throughout the Gospel of Luke and much of Acts, Luke gives a third person account of what he observed in the life and ministry of Jesus and his followers. However, in Acts 16, something remarkable happens to Luke which is simply noted in the change of a pronoun:

> *Then coming to the borders of Mysia, they headed for the province of Bithynia, but again the Spirit of Jesus did not let them go. So instead, they went on through Mysia to the city of Troas.*
>
> *That night, Paul had a vision. He saw a man from Macedonia in northern Greece, pleading with him, "Come over here and help us." So WE decided to leave for Macedonia at once, for WE could only conclude that God was calling Us to preach the Good News there.*
>
> **Acts 16:6-10 NLT**

When we step in the stream, "they" becomes "we."

After years of being a passionate observer, Luke became an obedient servant and personally joined the journey of faith. From the text, we do not know what triggered Luke to make this shift. All we know is that he tells when he personally chose to step into the stream with the others.

Like Luke, many of us spend many years and may even dedicate many hours of observing, or even serving, from the bank of the stream. And yet, like Luke, there comes a time when, in full obedience to God, we must choose to step in with both feet. When we do so, we join the other travellers on this journey of faith and we commit ourselves to bringing about the Kingdom of God here on earth. That is when THEY becomes WE, and our story is woven into the grand history of God's people.

Each ministry and church becomes another tributary into the mighty River of God.

The Command to Tell

Since the Exodus story, when God began FORMING us as a called people, God has commanded us to tell the story of WHO God is and WHAT God has done in our lives. On the night before the Israelites were to begin their journey out of Egypt, God called them to celebrate the Passover as a way of remembering WHO God was, WHO they were as God's people, and WHAT God was doing for them.

> *Remember, these instructions are permanent and must be observed by you and your descendents forever. When you arrive in the land the LORD has promised to give you, you will continue to celebrate this festival. Then your children will ask, "What does all this mean? What is this ceremony about?" And you will reply, "It is the celebration of the LORD's Passover, for he passed over the homes of the Israelites in Egypt. And though he killed the Egyptians, he spared our families and did not destroy us."*
>
> **Exodus 12:24-27** NLT

To this day, when the Jewish people gather together to celebrate the Passover, one of the youngest ones present at the table asks the question, "What makes this night different from all others?" And each time, an older member answers with the retelling of the story so they can remember WHO God is, WHO they are as God's people, and WHAT God has done for them.

Likewise, on the night before Jesus was to take the journey to the cross, he gathered his disciples together for a shared meal and said:

> *"I have looked forward to this hour with deep longing, anxious to eat this Passover meal with you before my suffering begins. For I tell you now that I won't eat it again until it comes to fulfillment in the Kingdom of God."*
>
> *Then he took the cup of wine, and when he had given thanks for it, he said, "Take this and share it among yourselves. For I will not drink wine again until the Kingdom of God has come."*
>
> *Then he took a loaf of bread; and when he had thanked God for it, he broke it in pieces and gave it to the disciples saying, "This is my body, given for you. Do this in remembrance of me." After supper, he took another cup of wine and said, "This wine is the token of God's new covenant to save you—an agreement sealed with the blook I will pour out for you."*
>
> **Luke 22:15-20 NLT**

To this day we gather as often as we can to celebrate Communion, or the Lord's Supper. And through the words spoken in the Prayer of Great Thanksgiving, we tell The Story of WHO God is, WHO we are as God's people, and WHAT God has done for us through Jesus Christ.

A Meal of Remembrance and Preparation

In both the Passover meal and the Lord's Supper, we are to gather around a shared meal to tell The Story and to remember how our stories as a community of faith are woven into it. And although both Passover and Communion are meals to remember our history, they were also both instituted by God to prepare us for the future Kingdom to which God is calling us. In the sharing of these sacred meals and in the weaving together of The Story with our stories, we begin to understand where we were in our past, how we arrived in the present, and we begin to envision the future where God desires us to go.

As we FORM as a group called together for God's purpose, it is essential that we, too, set aside the sacred time and space (through a shared meal and even Communion) to tell The Story and to share how our individual stories are woven together in the history of God's people. In the weaving together of our stories with The Story, we are reminded WHO we are, WHOSE we are, and WHAT God has done for us in the past. In the sharing of our history, as a church, as a ministry, and as individuals, our present is better explained. And once we understand how we got to where we are today, we can better understand where God intends to take us tomorrow.

Every believer and every church represent another tributary that converges and flows together into the stream of God's will. As our faith journeys, callings, and stories converge, they will become the mighty River of God that will bring healing and restoration to all the nations.

> *Then the angel showed me the river of the water of life, bright as crystal, flowing from the throne of God and of the Lamb through the middle of the street of the city. On either side of the river is the tree of life with its twelve kinds of fruit, producing its fruit each month; and the leaves of the*

tree are for the healing of the nations.
Revelation 22:1-2 NRSV

This is the will of God—that we, together, become instruments
of healing for this broken and hurting world. God's good,
pleasing, and perfect will is fulfilled one tributary, one step at a
time with the history of God's faithful people flowing together.
When we pause to weave our stories with The Story, the past can
begin to inform our present, and through the sanctifying work of
the Holy Spirit, God will transform us for the future.

Questions for Discussion

To be used in conjunction with your timeline and sharing your history.

1. How does our history inform us in Who we are, Whose we are, or How we got to where we are today?

2. How have we let go of the past to grab hold of God's promising future—or not?

3. When and how have we "stepped in the stream" by faith?

4. How have we witnessed God at work through our history?

5. When did we each choose to join in this journey of faith?

The Right Next Step for Chapter Four

At the end of every chapter are daily Scripture readings and prayer guides. Set aside at least fifteen minutes every day to seek the Scriptures and pray as you ask for God's clarity in the vision for your ministry.

Read the Scriptures and pray with your heart and mind open and expecting God to speak.

Keep a journal or notes of ways in which God may be speaking to you. Share these with one another as you come together.

Scripture & Prayers

Day 1
Ecclesiastes 3:1 & 11
There is a time for everything, a season for every activity under heaven.

God has made everything beautiful for its own time. He has planted eternity in the human heart, but even so, people cannot see the whole scope of God's work from beginning to end.
NLT

Focus Notes

Psalm 78:2-4
I will open my mouth in a parable; I will utter dark sayings from of old, things that we have heard and known, that our ancestors have told us. We will not hide them from their children; we will tell to the coming generation the glorious deeds of the Lord, and his might, and the wonders that he has done.
NRSV

Lord, help me remember that I am on journey to fulfill your will. Help me remember the past, the wonders you have done and your faithfulness. Do not let me long for the past, but help me live in the present and look with hope to the future. Teach me how to see your hand at work in time and to trust you for the future. Thank you for not leaving me in the past and for transforming me daily for the future.

Day 2
Mark 1:16-17
One day as Jesus was walking along the shores of the Sea of Galilee, he saw Simon and his brother, Andrew, fishing with a net, for they were commercial fishermen. Jesus called out to them, "Come, be my disciples, and I will show you how to fish for people!" NLT

Focus Notes

Jesus, you would never call me to be someone other than who you created me to be. You have prepared me to operate within and for your kingdom just as I operate here on earth. Help me remember my identity in you and my calling by you. Let my work flow from my calling as your disciple and from my past preparation as one set apart for your Kingdom.

Day 3
Revelation 2:4-5
Yet I have this against you: You have forsaken your first love. Remember the height from which you have fallen! Repent and do the thing you did at first. NIV

Jesus, help me overcome the past. Let me not dwell there and let me not repeat the sins of the past. I want to move forward boldly and unashamed to the glorious future you have prepared for me. Help me remember daily who I am, whose I am, and what I have been called to do. I want you to be my First Love and my reason for being.

Day 4
Luke 9:62
Jesus said to him, "No one who puts a hand to the plow and looks back is fit for the kingdom of God." NRSV

Focus Notes

2 Corinthians 5:7
We live by faith, not by sight. NIV

Lord Jesus, You did not promise that our walk of faith would be an easy one. We do not want to yearn for the past or doubt once we have committed our lives to you. We want to plow straight and deep rows for your Kingdom. Help us to keep our eyes fixed on you and forward, remembering that our reward is in heaven. Let us not be discouraged by what we see or can't see, but trust in the eternal unseen. Lord, we believe, help our unbelief.

Day 5
Matthew 10:38-39
And unless you are willing to take up your cross and come with me, you are not fit to be my disciples. If you try to save your life, you will lose it. But if you give it up for me, you will surely find it. CEV

Jesus, I want to be worthy of you. The cost to follow you is every-thing...my desires, my ambition, my will. I must die to "self." Help me to see what a glorious death that is. I want to crucify my human fleshly nature and step without fear into your will and your promises. Help me to see that this is truly the only place where I will find true Joy and Peace. Help me be a living sacrifice, Jesus.

Focus Notes

Day 6
Joshua 3:8, 15-16
Tell the priests who carry the Ark of the Covenant: "When you reach the edge of the Jordan's waters, go stand in the river."

Now the Jordan was at flood stage all during the harvest. Just as soon as the priests who carried the ark reached the Jordan and their feet touched the water's edge, the water from upstream stopped flowing.... NIV

Mighty God, my journey and my obedience are not just a part of a personal journey but a corporate journey. Other people's lives are being changed and affected by my willingness to step into your stream. Other people's lives will be changed forever by my willingness to obey or disobey. Help me to see that it is not about me, but about "us."

Day 7
Psalm 46:4
A river brings joy to the city of our God, the sacred home of the Most High. NLT

Malachi 3:16-17
Then those who feared the Lord talked with each other, and the Lord listened and heard. A scroll of remembrance was written in his presence concerning those who feared the Lord and honored his name. "They will be mine," says the Lord, "in the day when I make up my treasured possession." NIV

Father, Son, and Holy Spirit, let our voices and songs of you be like a mighty river that flows to you and then from you to all nations, tribes, and tongues. Give us tongues of blessing and not cursing, joy and not dismay, love and not hate, life and not death. We want a scroll of remembrance to be written about us: One that speaks of obedience and joy in doing your will and one that honors and glorifies your holy name.

Trust in the Lord
with all your heart;
do not depend
on your own
understanding.
Seek his will
in all you do,
And he will direct
your paths.

Proverbs 3:5-6

Four

Getting in the Stream—And Staying There

*A*s baptized believers in Jesus Christ, we have all been called to a common purpose: to fulfill the will of God. Fulfilling the will of God, however, requires our doing what God wants us to do but not necessarily what we want to do. There is a distinct difference between implementing our good ideas and being about the will of God. The former relies on our own prowess, whereas the latter relies on the power of God.

The Ministry of Moses

Throughout the book of Exodus, we hear the story of Moses, a man who was unabashedly committed to fulfilling the will of God. From releasing the people from bondage to bordering the Promised Land, Moses demonstrated an unwavering commitment to God's purpose for his people. Even though Moses was no doubt gifted and skilled, it was his obedience to God's will that defined his life and ministry. There were undoubtedly many times when Moses would have rather taken a different path if not a different group of people! But instead, Moses submitted his own wants to the will of God and faithfully led the people through.

Moses clearly demonstrated his skill as a competent leader, and yet he followed closely the leading of God. Repeatedly, Scripture reflects that Moses completed each task *just as the LORD commanded*. In Exodus 40, we hear about Moses following and giving specific instructions based on God's explicit desires for completion of the Tabernacle from the placement of the Ark to the washing of their feet. Moses may have had his own ideas or even preferences for how the Tabernacle was to be constructed, set up, or operated. If we were Moses, we might have even argued that "after all we've done" we deserved to have some say in the matter. However, in full obedience to God's will, Moses adhered to God's instructions for the Tabernacle down to the smallest detail.

> *Moses proceeded to do everything as the LORD commanded him. So the Tabernacle was set up on the first day of the new year. Moses put it together by setting its frames into their bases and attaching the crossbars and raising the posts. Then he spread the coverings over the Tabernacle framework and put on the roof layer, just as the LORD had commanded him.*
>
> *He placed inside the Ark the stone tablets inscribed with the terms of the covenant, and then he attached the Ark's carrying poles. He also set the Ark's cover—the place of atonement—on top of it. Then he brought the Ark of the Covenant into the Tabernacle and set up the inner curtain to shield it from view, just as the LORD had commanded.*

Exodus 40:16-21 NLT

Not My Will, but Thine

Jesus' life and ministry were also distinctively defined by obedience and submission to God's will. The disciples asked Jesus what God wanted them to do. Jesus responded by telling them what he had come to do:

> *I didn't come from heaven to do what I want! I came to do what the Father wants me to do. He sent me, and he wants to make certain that none of the ones he has given me will be lost. Instead, he wants me to raise them to life on the last day. My Father wants everyone who sees the Son to have faith in him and to have eternal life. Then I will raise them to life on the last day*

John 6:38-40 CEV

Even though he was the Son of God, Jesus did not operate independently from God. Instead, he conformed his will to the will of his Father—even when it cost him his life.

> *Father, if you are willing, please take this cup of suffering away from me. Yet I want your will, not mine.*

Luke 22:42 NLT

In the face of suffering and even death, Jesus submitted his own desire to God's. Jesus likewise taught his followers to pray:

> *Your kingdom come, your will be done on earth, as it is in heaven.*

Matthew 6:10 NIV

Our purpose, like Moses and Jesus, must be to fulfill God's purpose. Therefore, we should not be driven by human wants and desires, not even our own. Instead, we are called to lay aside, or sacrifice, our own agendas for the sake of the agenda of God.

> *And so, dear brothers and sisters, I plead with you to give your bodies to God. Let them be a living and holy sacrifice— the kind he will accept. When you think of what he has done for you, is this too much to ask? Don't copy the behavior and customs of this world, but let God transform you into a new person by changing the way you think. Then you will know what God wants you to do, and you will know how good and pleasing and perfect his will really is.*

Romans 12:1-2 NLT

As we attempt to shape our work and ministry, the temptation to copy the behaviors and customs of the world is powerful. If we are motivated to do those things that will puff us up and earn us accolades in the eyes of others, we greatly jeopardize our obedience to the will of God. To step into the stream of God's will requires letting go of our own agenda to trust God's agenda, even if it is radically different from what we, or others, had in mind.

The only way our ministries will be acceptable to God is by letting God transform how we think about them. Submitting our ministries to God's design and direction (and placing our resources at God's disposal) is the only way our work will be for God's glory and not our own.

From Good Ideas to God's Ideas

The transition from implementing our good ideas to discerning what is God's idea is an intentional process involving seeking to know and understand God's will and to let go of what we have always known.

> *Trust in the Lord with all your heart;*
> *Do not depend on your own understanding.*
> *Seek his will in all you do,*
> *And he will direct your paths.*

Proverbs 3:5-6 NLT

When we seek to understand God's ideas and plans, we must first learn to think and listen a whole new way—to listen with our ears, our eyes, our hearts, and our minds. In Scripture, we see examples of God speaking directly to individuals like Abraham, Moses, David and the prophets. And in these conversations the will of God was spoken directly to the individuals. Even in Acts, we hear that the Holy Spirit spoke to Paul and Silas to direct their path:

> *They went through the region of Phrygia and Galatia, having been forbidden by the Holy Spirit to speak the word in Asia. When they had come opposite Mysia, they attempted to go into Bithynia, but the Spirit of Jesus did not allow them; so, passing by Mysia, they went down to Troas.*

Acts 16:6-8 NRSV

Even today, we occasionally hear God's voice or know the leading of the Spirit. And yet at other times, we can not hear a clear leading from God. When traveling on an unfamiliar route, nothing is more frustrating than a lack of clear direction and signs. Likewise, it is incredibly frustrating when we want to do God's will but have no clear direction on what is the right next step to take.

Stop and Ask

To find God's right path we must stop and ask!

At one time or another, we've all experienced it: we set out on a journey knowing the final destination, but we don't have clear directions on how to get there. We take a wrong turn here. We wonder if we were supposed to turn there? And then it finally becomes obvious that we're lost! But the real dilemma is this: Do we keep wandering on our own until we hopefully find it, or do we stop and ask?

Despite all the jokes, it's not really a gender issue. The real issue is whether or not we will admit our own need for direction and submit to the leading of another. There comes a point where we must stop and ask for directions and then listen attentively for the answer. We must cut off the radio, silence the other voices in the car, and listen intently to the one who can guide us along the right path.

> ***Teach me to do your will, for you are my God. May your gracious Spirit lead me forward on a firm foundation.***
> **Psalm 143:10 NLT**

We must listen to God leading us along the right path so we can avoid making wrong turns. But hearing God's voice does not usually happen accidentally in the chaotic, noisy world in which we live. To know God's will requires creating the right environment that allows God's voice to break through the clatter and distractions all around us. We must be trained to hear God's voice with our ears, eyes, hearts, and minds. We must embrace discipline—spiritual discipline—to be transformed by and conformed to the will of God and to remain on God's right path.

Long Distance Discipline

As mentioned earlier, stepping and living into the stream of God's will is a life-long journey which will not be completed on this side of eternity. Long distance runners know that we must be well-trained and disciplined not only to complete the race but to overcome the various obstacles we will encounter. The same is true for our spiritual journey. To follow and fulfill the will of God, we must practice the spiritual disciplines allowing them to inform us and conform us to God's will.

> *Spiritual disciplines inform us and conform us to God's will.*

John Wesley, the founder of the Methodist movement, was convinced that a life of faith lived in obedience must be grounded in the spiritual disciplines. However, Wesley also warned that the practice of the disciplines was not what would make us obedient or more like Christ. Only God's grace can do that! However, the spiritual disciplines, or the means of grace, are the ways by which we open ourselves and our ministries to be transformed into the likeness of Christ and conformed to the will of God.

Practicing the Means of Grace

Wesley described the means of grace as ordinary practices, or activities, we do on a regular basis to place ourselves in the right place at the right time for God to break through to us and in us. Another way to think about spiritual disciplines is what defines our Sabbath moments. These "breathing in" practices include searching the Scriptures, prayer, fasting, the Lord's Supper, Christian conferencing, and public worship.

Searching the Scriptures

The primary way to know the will of God is to read the Word of God. From Genesis to Revelation, Scripture reveals the character and nature of who God is and God's desire that all should be brought into a saving relationship through Jesus Christ. Scripture also provides clear instruction for our lives. It should serve as the primary measuring tool, or plumb line, by which all things in our lives and ministries are measured.

> *All scripture is inspired by God and is useful to teach us what is true and to make us realize what is wrong in our lives. It straightens us out and teaches us to do what is right. It is God's way of preparing us in every way, fully equipped for every good thing God wants us to do.*
>
> **2 Timothy 3:16-17 NLT**

God's will is always consistent with God's Word.

Because of the centrality of Scripture in a life of obedience to God's will, John Wesley in his *Explanatory Notes Upon the New Testament* offered six practical suggestions for how to apply Scripture to our lives and ministries:

1. **Set apart time in the morning and/or evening every day to read your Bible.**

2. **Read from both the Old and New Testaments every day.**

3. **Read scripture with a single purpose—to know the will of God.**

4. **Look for connections between the scriptures being read to identify the ideas essential to our life of faith.**

5. **Prayerfully ask the Holy Spirit to guide you and instruct you as you read the scriptures.**

6. **Commit to put into practice right away what God is teaching you in his Word.**

As we commit ourselves to following God's path for us, we must constantly seek wisdom and direction that is offered to us when we read God's Word.

Your word is a lamp for my feet and light for my path.
Psalm 119:105 NLT

Prayer

What an awesome reality that the Creator of the universe wants to communicate with us. Prayer opens another channel through which God speaks to us and we can speak to God as we seek to know and fulfill the purpose for our existence. Prayer offers a primary means through which we stay connected with and near to God. And yet without this line of communication, we are at great risk of being disconnected and getting way off course.

Prayer opens us to God speaking to us and through us.

In the book of Acts, we hear that one of the key activities that bound the believers together was their private and communal prayers. In the first chapter of Acts, the apostles were faced with their first crucial decision as a group of believers—the replacement of Judas:

Then they all prayed for the right man to be chosen. "O Lord,"
they said, "you know every heart. Show us which of these
men you have chosen as an apostle to replace Judas.
Acts 1:24-25 NLT

Although these men had been together for over three years and
probably knew one another and the other followers very well,
they did not look to their own opinions or preferences to make
this decision. Instead, they looked to the Lord, trusting that he
alone knew what was best and trusting that the Lord would show
them through prayer.

When we pray both individually and corporately for God's
will to be made known, we open ourselves even further to God
speaking to us and through us in the context of prayer. Especially
when we are in desperate need of help but don't have the words
to express it, placing ourselves in the posture and attitude of
prayer can be sufficient as a means of receiving God's grace and
guidance.

Likewise the Spirit helps us in our weakness; for we do not
know how to pray as we ought, but that very Spirit inter-
cedes with sighs too deep for words. And God, who searches
the heart, knows what is the mind of the Spirit, because the
Spirit intercedes for the saints according to the will of God.
Romans 8:26-27 NRSV

To discern the will of God, we must listen to the voice of
God, and prayer, especially in combination with searching
the Scriptures, can be a powerful vessel through which God
speaks. Through God's Word, God speaks. In prayer, we can
open ourselves to listening and responding in adoration,
confession, thanksgiving, and supplication. Open, honest, and
ongoing communication is essential in a trusting relationship.
Therefore, we must openly, honestly, and daily pray to nurture

our relationship with God. In prayer, we not only step into the stream, but we also learn to trust God to take us where God wants us to go.

Fasting

Fasting, or the practice of abstaining from food, drink, or other things, is another means by which we can experience the grace and presence of God. By intentionally drawing away from something else for a period of time, we can draw nearer to God. Whether we give up food for a day

We fast to focus less on our wants and more on God's desires.

each week or television for a certain time each month, fasting is a way of diverting our desire for earthly things to setting our affections on the will of God.

The purpose of fasting as a means of grace, however, is less about self denial and more about focus on God and God's will. Fasting, like all other spiritual disciplines, is for the explicit purpose of drawing us closer to the likeness of Christ and to the will of God.

> *You even get angry and ready to fight. No wonder God won't listen to your prayers! Do you think the LORD wants you to give up eating and to act as humble as a bent-over bush? Or to dress in sackcloth and sit in ashes? Is this really what he wants on a day of worship?*
> *I'll tell you what it really means to worship the LORD. Remove the chains of prisoners who are chained unjustly. Free those who are abused! Share your food with everyone who is hungry; share your home with the poor and homeless. Give clothes to those in need; don't turn away your relatives Then your light will shine like the dawning sun, and you will quickly be healed. Your honesty will protect you as you*

91

advance, and the glory of the LORD will defend you from be-
hind. When you beg the LORD for help, he will answer, Here
I am!" Don't mistreat others or falsely accuse them
or say something cruel.

Isaiah 58:4-9 CEV

When we focus on God's will in and through our fasting, we
learn to let go of those things that oppress us and others and to
cling to Jesus Christ who will heal, lead, and protect us. To fast is
to focus not on our own wants but on the desires of God.

The Lord's Supper

Again in the book of Acts, we hear that the believers came
together as often as they could to share
in the Lord's Supper (Acts 2:43-47).

Communion
reminds us WHO we
are, WHOSE we are
and WHY we are
being sent.

But why? For many of us, we can
hardly imagine participating in the
Lord's Supper, or Communion, more
than once a month. And yet for the
early Christians, as for some believers
today, the Lord's Supper was a
powerful reminder of WHO they were
and WHOSE they were, and WHY they
had been sent.

For every time you eat this bread and drink this cup,
you are announcing the Lord's death until he comes again.

1 Corinthians 11:26 NLT

We are believers sent to re-present the One who died and rose
again to offer healing and hope to a broken and hurting world.
But unless we are reminded regularly of his redemptive death
and resurrection, we tend to fall back into the brokenness and
hopelessness of the world around us.

By sharing in Communion as often as we can, we are constantly reminded WHO we are, WHOSE we are, and WHY we are sent. In the Communion liturgy, we pray:

"Pour out your Holy Spirit on us gathered here and on these gifts of bread and wine. Make them be for us the body and blood of Christ, that we may be for the world the body of Christ redeemed by his blood.

By your Spirit, make us one with Christ, one with each other, and one in ministry to all the world, until Christ comes in final victory, and we feast at his heavenly banquet." (United Methodist Hymnal, 14)

When we regularly partake in the Lord's Supper, we are receiving a promise of God's convincing, converting, and sanctifying grace. Additionally, we are confirming our promise to God that we will actively participate in bringing about God's will until we feast together in Kingdom of God with Jesus.

To stay in the Stream we need both support and accountability.

Christian Conferencing

Even though spiritual growth is a personal commitment, it was never intended to be a private affair. We must each individually decide whether or not to take part in this journey of living into God's will. However, God calls us to live out this journey in the context of community.

The early Christians obviously knew the importance of coming together for support in their faith as they met together constantly (Acts 2:42-47). John Wesley also understood the need for Christian support and accountability among believers. He called this Christian conferencing and described its practice in *The*

Nature, Design, and General Rules of the United Societies written in 1743. People in the early Methodist movement were organized into small groups, or bands, for holy fellowship and conversation that both supported and held accountable all participants. These groups met weekly to:

1. **See each person in [the] class once a week at the least; in order to receive what they are willing to give toward the relief of the poor.**

2. **Inquire how their souls prosper.**

3. **Advise, reprove, comfort, and exhort, as occasion may require.**

4. **Inform the Minister of any that are sick, or of any that walk disorderly and will not be reproved.**

To step into the stream and to stay there, we need fellow sojourners of faith who will keep us true to our calling. The temptations to pull us out of God's will can be great, and we need to set apart sacred time and space to hold one another in the stream.

> *And let us consider how we may spur one another on toward love and good deeds. Let us not give up meeting together, as some are in the habit of doing, but let us encourage one another—and all the more as you see the Day approaching.*
> **Hebrews 10:24-25** NIV

True Christian conferencing is when we come together and speak the truth in love for the purpose of building up, and never tearing down one another so we can fulfill God's purpose among us. In this practice of regular, disciplined holy fellowship, God's grace is real, and God's will is made known.

Public Worship

What better way to submit to God's will than to humble ourselves before the Lord in worship? Coming into God's holy presence with hearts open is the way to know God and to dwell with God. Our private times of worship and praise are essential to our growing in intimacy with the Lord. However, public worship is also critical for us to be united in adoration and praise.

To be faithful Christians, our faith must be put into action through ministry and service that spiritually and practically changes the world. However, our action is only of God if it extends from God. Remember: our DOING for God must flow from our BEING with God.

> *How good it is to sing praises to our God!*
> *How delightful and how right!...*
> *The strength of a horse does not impress him;*
> *How puny in his sight is the strength of a man.*
> *Rather the Lord's delight is in those who honor him,*
> *those who put their hope in his unfailing love.*
> **Psalm 147:1 & 10 NLT**

Public worship grounds us in Jesus and binds us to one another.

Public worship is a vessel through which God's unlimited and unmerited love is poured out on us and where we gather to pour out our love on God. Public worship, especially in conjunction with the other spiritual disciplines, grounds us in Jesus Christ and binds us to one another. Our ministries for Jesus are defined by our corporate worship of him. Worship is the attitude behind the action. It is the WHY we do WHAT we do.

95

Getting in the Stream–and Staying There

When we commit ourselves, individually and corporately, to fulfilling the will of God, we choose to step into the stream—and stay there. We choose to lay aside our own agendas to flow in the agenda of God. However, we cannot even find the stream, much less stay in it, without a disciplined life that keeps us in relationship with Jesus Christ and one another.

To be part of a thriving ministry for Jesus, we must be in a thriving relationship with him. Otherwise, our ministry is all about us and will not bring glory to God. Apart from a vital relationship with Jesus Christ, we cannot ultimately bear any fruit for the sake of God, the Gardener, or the Kingdom.

> *Those who remain in me, and I in them, will produce much fruit. For apart from me you can do nothing.*
>
> **John 15:5** NLT

Committed practice of the spiritual disciplines keeps us connected to Jesus, the Vine, so we can produce fruit that will reflect the Kingdom of God. We must commit ourselves to searching the Scriptures, prayer, fasting, the Lord's Supper, Christian conferencing, and public worship to know, understand, and fulfill the will of God and to bring glory to the Gardener.

Fulfilling the will of God begins with one step—an intentional step into the stream. However, to ensure that we get and stay in the stream, we must intentionally practice the spiritual disciplines. To know, understand and fulfill God's will, we have been given these means of grace. Committed practice of the spiritual disciplines gets us in the stream and keeps us there.

Questions for Discussion

1. In what ways have we laid aside our own agendas to adhere to the agenda of God?
2. How have we copied the behaviors of the world instead of conforming to the will of God?
3. How has God spoken to us through Scripture and prayer?

The Right Next Step for Chapter Five

Read the following Scriptures to prepare for developing a relational covenant for your group:
- Philippians 2:3-8
- Ephesians 4:25-32
- Colossians 3:8-15
- 1 Corinthians 13:4-7
- Matthew 18:15-20

Take note of the essential biblical behaviors and attitudes that should define and protect your relationships and ministries together.

After reading Chapter Five come prepared to write a relational covenant together.

Note: Sample relational covenants are available in Appendix A or at www.steppinginthestream.org.

Scripture & Prayers
Day 1
Exodus 40:16
…as the Lord commanded him [Moses].

Exodus 40:34-35
Then the cloud covered the Tent of meeting and the glory of the Lord filled the tabernacle. Moses could not enter the tent because…the glory of the Lord filled the tabernacle. NIV

<table>
<tr><td>Focus Notes</td></tr>
</table>

Lord, help me see that obedience is the key to joy in my ministry. Help the church to see that obedience is the key to seeing your glory. When we walk in complete obedience to you, you come and dwell among us. You fill the place of your dwelling. Help us do as you command us so that we might see your glory in our lives and in our churches.

Day 2
Psalm 40:8-9
I delight to do your will, O my God; your law is within my heart." I have told the glad news of deliverance in the great congregation; see, I have not restrained my lips, as you know, O Lord. NRSV

My purpose and call, O God, is to do your will. Make it not just my purpose but my desire. Let your law transform my heart and my mind in accordance with your desires and not my own. Help me to be a living sacrifice for you. By doing so, I proclaim righteousness not just with my tongue, but also with my life. Help me demonstrate daily the submission of my will to your perfect will.

Day 3
Psalm 32:8
The LORD says, "I will guide you along the best pathway for your life. I will advise you and watch over you. NLT

Psalm 27:7-8
Please listen when I pray!
Have pity. Answer my prayer.
My heart tells me to pray.
I am eager to see your face.
CEV

Lord, teach me and help me to seek you for direction and counsel. You know the right way and the best way. You promise to teach me and watch over me as you guide me. Remind me that your way is the safest and most direct route even though I can not see. Let my heart be one that wants to seek your face, for in your presence I am trans-formed and my will is transformed to yours.

> **Focus Notes**

Day 4
Daniel 10:11-12
And then the angel said, "Daniel, your God thinks highly of you,

and he has sent me. So stand up and pay close attention." I stood trembling, while the angel said: "Daniel, don't be afraid! God has listened to your prayers since the first day you humbly asked for understanding, and he has sent me here." CEV

Lord, you hear our prayers when we humble ourselves before you. When we seek you for understanding, you are listening. Help me to seek you more and more in prayer. Teach me to listen more and speak less. Help me persevere when it seems that you are silent. I know you are perfecting your plans for me and for the Church. Help me not grow weary but to press on. Thank you, Jesus that you live to intercede for me when I am weary. I shall not forget that I have a Great High Priest in heaven.

Focus Notes

Day 5
Acts 13:2
While they were worshipping the Lord and fasting, the Holy Spirit said, "Set apart for me Barnabas and Saul for the work to which I have called them." NIV

Lord, when we focus our time and attention on you, you respond. When we let go of the physical and mental desires that keep us from you, we are then able to hear your Spirit speak. Give me the grace to fast those things that limit your Holy Sprit. Help me know when you are calling me to fast or let go, and seek you. Not my will or desires, but yours, O Lord.

Day 6
Psalm 32:10-11
Many are the torments of the wicked, but steadfast love surrounds those who trust in the Lord. Be glad in the Lord and rejoice, O righteous, and shout for joy, all you upright in heart. NRSV

To worship, O God, is why we were created. You surround us with your unfailing love. Help us see the power of our worship. It binds us to you and to one another. Our worship as the Body opens the way for you to act and move among us. Help us remember that we "enter your gates with thanksgiving and your courts with praise." We give thanks to you, Lord, and bless your name!

Day 7
Acts 2:46-47
Day after day they met together in the temple. They broke bread together in different homes and shared their food happily and freely, while praising God. Everyone liked them, and each day the Lord added to their group others who were being saved. CEV

Lord, help us remember that we need one another to stay true to your will and the plan for us. We need one another to discern your will for us as a body. You intended for us to grow and live out our Christian walk in community. There is truly safety and care in Christian fellowship. Help us each see the power, blessing, and witness of Christian fellowship and its impact on the Body, the individual, and the world. The early Christians gathered together and so today we gather together. Keep us true to their example. We praise you for their witness. Let our witness be as powerful.

Trust in the Lord
with all your heart;
do not depend
on your own
understanding.
Seek his will
in all you do,
And he will direct
your paths.
Proverbs 3:5-6

Five

Navigating the Storms

In the first four chapters, we have established that stepping into the stream of God's will is a communal faith journey in which our final "destination" is the fulfillment of the Kingdom of God. It is a journey of faith and obedience that requires our listening intently to God as we get in and remain in the stream. It is also a communal journey that requires our coming together for the shared purpose of fulfilling God's will among us.

As we discussed in Chapter One, this journey is a process that involves four different phases through which we will cycle as a community. In the last three chapters, we have explored the FORMING phase of this process where we learn WHO we are and WHOSE we are as a group called together to fulfill a common purpose. In FORMING as a group, we learn to dwell first and foremost with God then with one another. And through the practice of the spiritual disciplines, we begin to discern the voice and will of God. We begin to connect our own stories with the unfolding Story of God's people as we commit ourselves to stepping in the stream of God's will.

Conflict, or STORMING, is natural, inevitable, and important in our ministries together.

When we FORM as a group, we cast the sea anchor that steadies us as people who belong to Jesus Christ and one another and who are commited to bringing about God's Kingdom. The sea anchor is essential to weather the inevitable STORMS we will encounter on this journey. Because every relationship—and every journey—involves rocky roads and slippery slopes. Every jouney of faith involves clashes of views, opinions, wishes, needs and desires. In fact, conflict, or STORMING, is inevitable and even important in defining and refining our identity and function. And although the conflict itself does not harm us as a group, how we respond to the conflict can. The key, therefore, is not avoiding the conflict but rather knowing how to weather the STORMS in ways that maintain the integrity of our relationships and ministries.

Storming Through the Ages

Throughout the history of God's people, we have repeatedly stormed as we have defined and refined WHO we are and WHAT God is calling us to Do. Our history also shows us that the more we step out in faith, opposition and fear move in.

Submitting to God's will requires an openness to change, and pending change often triggers resistance and fear. As humans, what we frequently fear the most is the unknown—that wide open abyss filled with constant questions and delayed answers. The process of stepping into the stream involves going where God wants us to go, even if it is into unknown and uncharted territory. Nonetheless, facing new territories and tasks can evoke fear and distrust in one another and even in God.

> *Stepping in the stream involves going into unknown and even uncharted territory.*

The Exodus out of Egypt into the Promised Land was one such journey. Although the promise of God was articulated for them, they still couldn't see it, understand it, and especially couldn't control it. The journey required their taking one step at a time into unfamiliar circumstances and surroundings.

God, of course, was completely aware of the fear this journey would evoke. As a result, Moses and the people were promised God's continual presence and God even altered the course of the journey to lessen the impact of their fear.

> *When Pharaoh finally let the people go, God did not lead them on the road that runs through Philistine territory, even though that was the shortest way from Egypt to the Promised Land. God said, "If the people are faced with a battle, they might change their minds and return to Egypt." So God led them along a route through the wilderness toward the Red Sea.*

> **Exodus 13:17-18 NLT**

In this way the long wilderness journey began according to God's plan. God had changed the route to minimize anxiety, and yet the first day into the journey, the fear and tempers flared.

> *As Pharaoh approached, the Israelites looked up, and there were the Egyptians, marching after them. They were terrified and cried out to the LORD. They said to Moses, "Was it because there were no graves in Egypt that you brought us to the desert to die? What have you done to us by bringing us out of Egypt? Didn't we say to you in Egypt, 'Leave us alone; let us serve the Egyptians'? It would have been better for us to serve the Egyptians than to die in the desert!"*

> **Exodus 14:10-12 NIV**

Just a few days ago, this plan of promise sounded so good, then they were faced with opposition, and the fear kicked in. Immediately, the same group that was unified in moving forward was now opposed to Moses and wanted to go back. God, Moses, and the people now had differing views, opinions, wishes, needs, and desires about the destination and the course of this journey.

And thus the STORMING began.

Throughout the books of Exodus and Numbers, we hear STORMING among God's people. This storming is known as the murmuring tradition—a tradition still practiced in our churches today! When we submit to doing God's will, we must relinquish control. But as soon as our circumstances start to feel "out of control," we tend to turn on the leadership and one another. What initially seemed like a good plan starts to look like a big mistake made by someone else. As a result, we start to sound like the Israelites convening the "Back to Egypt" committee:

> *We need biblical relational boundaries so we can articulate our hopes and fears.*

"Why did they get us into this situation?"

"We tried to tell them it wouldn't work."

"We've never done it that way before."

"We should go back to the way things were."

Fear of the unknown, even fear of change, can be very real and even daunting. So, when the storms occur on our journey, how do we stay in the stream and avoid getting tossed out onto the shore?

The key to navigating the storms is having our sea anchor in place. Again, the sea anchor is our knowing and reflecting WHO we are and WHOSE we are by defining and protecting our relationships with Jesus Christ and one another. However, this does not necessarily come "naturally." We must intentionally embrace biblical skills that empower us to voice our fears and our needs so the obstacles on the journey can be identified and hopefully removed.

We must be committed to creating the sacred space and time where any and all of the group can give voice to both their hopes and fears on this journey so we can move forward together in faith. However, this is only possible if we know and practice these biblical skills and behaviors so that each person's voice is honored even if that voice differs from our own.

Biblical Skills for Healthy Storming

The following are essential biblical skills that will help us navigate through the storms. These skills include behaviors and attitudes that are essential to resolving conflict among us in ways that will strengthen, and not threaten, our life and ministry together.

Seek First to Understand

To remain in relationship with each other and to protect the integrity of our mission, we must have a true desire to understand one another. However, the practice of understanding requires a willingness to "stand under" the other person—the way a child must stand under other people.

We must seek first to understand one another before demanding to be understood.

Jesus called a small child over to him and put the child among them. Then he said, "I assure you, unless you turn from your sins and become as little children, you will never get into the Kingdom of Heaven. Therefore, anyone who becomes as humble as this little child is the greatest in the Kingdom of Heaven.

Matthew 18:2-4 NLT

Seeking to understand one another requires us to humble ourselves by no longer demanding what we think we deserve or what we think may be "right." Instead, we must lay down our

rights and privileges for the sake of the relationship and our
shared calling as a group together.

> *Don't be selfish; don't live to make a good impression on others. Be humble, thinking of others as better than yourself. Don't think only about your own affairs, but be interested in others, too, and what they are doing.*
>
> *Your attitude should be the same that Christ Jesus had. Though he was God, he did not demand and cling to his rights as God. He made himself nothing; he took the humble position of a slave and appeared in human form. And in human form, he obediently humbled himself even further by dying a criminal's death on a cross.*
>
> **Philippians 2:3-8** NLT

When we take on the posture and attitude of Jesus, we humbly
submit ourselves to fulfilling the will of God. By seeking to
understand the needs and opinions of God first then other
people, we don't demand that we be first heard and understood.
Additionally, we acknowledge that God's will may be spoken
through the thoughts and words of another as readily as it would
through us.

Speak the Truth in Love

To be and remain in relationship with each other and within the
stream of God's will, we must communicate honorably with one
another by speaking the truth in love. Communication, or the
ability to speak and listen in ways that are understood, is a special
gift to us from God used to nurture our relationships. So often,
however, we take this gift for granted, and we abuse the gift by
speaking dishonorably and irresponsibly.

We are warned about the power of our communication to bless
or curse our colleagues and our ministry:

Sometimes [the tongue] praises our Lord and Father, and sometimes it breaks out into curses against those who have been made in the image of God. And so blessing and cursing come pouring out of the same mouth. Surely, my brothers and sisters, this is not right!

James 3:9-10 NLT

In all our communications, we must make sure that our words always build up and never tear down one another or the group. And the only way to validate our words is to speak the truth from our own experience. The fullness of the truth, then, is only revealed when each person is allowed to speak for themselves from their own perspective. In this way, the truth comes forth when all the accounts are told, heard, and understood.

Our words should always build up and never tear down one another or our ministries.

The truth, however, is only edifying if it is spoken in an attitude of love. Speaking the truth is what we must do. Love is the reason, or the attitude, for doing it.

Love is kind and patient, never jealous, boastful, proud, or rude. Love isn't selfish or quick tempered. It doesn't keep a record of wrongs that others do. Love rejoices in the truth, but not in evil. Love is always supportive, loyal, hopeful, and trusting.

1 Corinthians 13:4-7 CEV

Even the truth, spoken out of bitterness, anger, or malice, can threaten individuals in the group and the group and ministry as a whole. Therefore, all of our communications must be spoken in an attitude of love.

Listen for the Truth in Love

It is not an accident that God gave us two ears and one mouth indicating that we should listen twice as much as we speak! So if we listen twice as much as we speak, healthy relationships will result. We must learn to practice a specific type of listening called active listening, and it should always be done in an attitude of love.

Active listening, like speaking the truth in love, involves engaging the heart, the mind, and ears together to listen for the truth. When we actively listen, we commit our full attention to both what is being said and how it is being said. We must listen for both the facts and the feelings to understand the fullness of the truth being spoken. But how can we be sure that we have understood what is really being said?

Reflective listening is the practice of reflecting back, or mirroring, that which we hear the other person saying including the facts and the feelings. Reflective listening is not merely echoing words, but rather rephrasing what we hear for the purpose of clarifying and understanding. So we listen, expecting to hear the truth, in an attitude of humility and love. In this way, we build greater trust, understanding, and harmony among us.

Move from the Incidents to the Issues

Once we learn to speak and listen for the purpose of truly understanding one another, the actual issues surrounding our struggles start to emerge. Too often, however, when we start telling our perspective of the struggle, we get stuck in the muck and the mire of what has happened in the past, and we never move on to deal with the real issues at hand. More importantly (and tragically), when we get stuck in the past, we cannot move forward in claiming God's promise for our future.

The reality is this: We can not change the incidents of the past, but we can change how we respond to the issues facing us today. Issues that have presented problems in the past typically present problems in the present and the future. Therefore, since we can not change the incidents of the past, we must focus on how to respond to the real issues before us. We must press on.

To see God's promise for our future, we have to get out of the slop bucket of the past!

> *Not that I have already obtained all this, or have already been made perfect, but I press on to take hold of that which Christ Jesus took hold of me. Brothers [and sisters], I do not consider myself yet to have taken hold of it. But one thing I do: Forgetting what is behind me and straining toward what is ahead, I press on toward the goal to win the prize for which God has called me heavenward in Christ Jesus.*
>
> **Philippians 3:12-14 NIV**

Unless we get our faces out of the "slop bucket" of the past, we will never be able to see the promising future God has in store. We must press on by refusing to go back to the "slop bucket" where we remind one another of past mistakes and failures. Instead, we strain toward the promising future ahead by seeking agreement on what really matters and letting go of that which doesn't.

Agree and Disagree in Love

As we press on to the promising future God has in store, we must learn to agree and disagree in an attitude of love. Expressing our different views, opinions, wishes, needs, and desires is natural among us as a group. Furthermore, it is essential in our understanding God's mission and vision for us and the values we must embrace to fulfill them. Therefore, we must learn to express our differing opinions in ways that build up and never tear down one another or the group.

In First Corinthians, Paul was addressing the church where many different opinions were emerging regarding their life and ministry together. As the opinions emerged, people spoke their minds but without considering how their words would affect one another. So opinions became arguments, and arguments became divisions. Their words were divided, and their hearts were divided, so eventually their church was also divided. In response to this division, Paul wrote:

> *Now, dear brothers and sisters, I appeal to you, by the authority of the Lord, Jesus Christ, to stop arguing among yourselves. Let there be real harmony so there won't be divisions in the church. I plead with you to be of one mind, united in thought and purpose.*

1 Corinthians 1:10 NLT

Our differing voices and opinions must be tuned to the common pitch of our mission and vision.

Paul does not say, "Don't disagree." Instead, he says, "Be of one mind, united in thought and purpose." Paul tells us to seek agreement or to have "real harmony" on that which really matters. What really matters is our life in Jesus Christ and the common mission and purpose to which he has called us.

For peace and harmony among us, we must agree on God's mission and vision for us (which defines that promising future), and yet we may differ on some matters of achieving it. The key is not allowing our differences to become divisive. We must seek "real harmony" by tuning our differing voices and opinions to the one common pitch of Jesus Christ and his mission and vision for his church.

Release and Reconcile

As the group attempts to live in harmony within the boundaries established by God, there are still times where we "miss the mark" with each other. The Greek word for sin means to miss the mark. Whether by inattention or intention, there are times when our words and our actions offend one another. And yet to maintain peace and unity among us, we must forgive one another as Christ Jesus has forgiven us.

As God's chosen ones, holy and beloved, clothe yourselves with compassion, kindness, humility, meekness, and patience. Bear with one another and, if anyone has a complaint against another, forgive each other; just as the Lord has forgiven you, so you also must forgive.

Colossians 3:12-13 NRSV

Since all of us will make mistakes and fail one another at some point on this journey, forgiveness is critical to our remaining in ministry together. Jesus knew clearly how important forgiveness would be in our staying in relationship and in ministry, and so he forgave us first so we can forgive one another. Furthermore, Jesus repeatedly taught us that because we are forgiven, we must forgive others without keeping track of how much or how often (Matthew 18:21-22).

To forgive the other person means to RELEASE them without any pre-existing conditions such as confession or repentance on the other person's part. To FORGIVE requires the major action by the one who has been offended. We must RELEASE the other person first by forgiving them (even BEFORE the offender even asks to be forgiven!). Paul reminds us that Jesus FORGAVE our sins *while we were YET sinners!* However, when we are unwilling or unable to RELEASE the one who has offended us, we are keeping ourselves in bondage to that person and to the offense that was committed.

When we "miss the mark," or offend one another, our BEING and DOING together may be threatened. Therefore, we must be reconciled for the sake of our relationship and our mission. To be reconciled in our relationships means to be in "right standing" with one another much like a checkbook is reconciled with a bank statement. To be reconciled, however, does not necessarily mean that we agree on all matters but rather that we agree on how the relationship stands in the context of our ministry, even if we have agreed to disagree in love.

Forgiveness = To Release

Reconciliation = To Restore

Jesus gave us clear instructions on handling conflict and offense within the community of the church. Here are his words:

> *"If another believer sins against you, go privately and point out the fault. If the other person listens and confesses it, you have won that person back. But if you are unsuccessful, take one or two others with you and go back again, so that everything you say may be confirmed by two or three witnesses. If that person still refuses to listen, take your case to the church. If the church decides you are right, but the other person won't accept it, treat that person as a pagan or a corrupt tax collector. I tell you this: Whatever you prohibit on earth is prohibited in heaven, and whatever you allow on earth is allowed in heaven."*
>
> *"I also tell you this: If two of you agree down here on earth concerning anything you ask, my Father in heaven will do it for you. For where two or three gather together because they are mine, I am there among them."*
>
> **Matthew 18:15-20 NLT**

The following is an outline of the key steps in the process for reconciliation Jesus taught us in Matthew 18:15-20:
REMEMBER: **Before reconciliation can take place, the offended must** FORGIVE **(or** RELEASE**) the one who offends them.** The following steps therefore, are to be taken for the relationship to be RESTORED into right standing:

1. FIRST, GO ONE-ON-ONE IN PRIVATE
If you have been offended by someone, you (the offended) must first go one-on-one in private to the person who has offended you to point out the offense and to seek first to understand the one who has offended you.
REMEMBER: The one who has been offended may be the ONLY one who knows that the offense has occurred. Therefore, reconciliation MUST begin with the OFFENDED taking the first step.

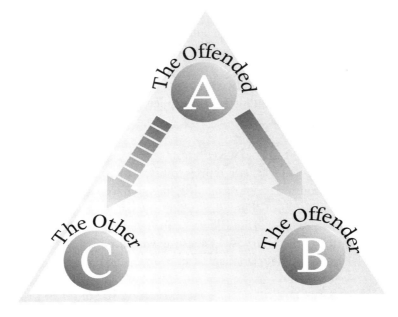

2. Avoid Triangulation

The offended (Party A) must go directly, in private, to the offender (Party B) and NOT to a third person (Party C) for reconciliation to take place. To tell Party C about the offense is to risk the sin of gossip which threatens greatly the health and functioning of the group and our ministry. If this happens, Party C should, in love, redirect Party A to go directly to Party B. REMEMBER: The only ones who can reconcile the relationship are Parties A and B. When other parties get involved without these two working together to heal the relationship, these two are forced further apart.

Triangulation, or gossip, greatly threatens the health and integrity of our ministries.

3. Take A Christian Witness With You

If after going one-on-one and the offender (Party B) does not hear or understand the nature of the offense, and if the relationship is not reconciled or "made in right standing," then the offended (Party A) takes one or two witnesses (who are committed to BOTH A AND B) to help them in their listening and understanding for the explicit purpose of Parties A and B being reconciled.

4. The Church Assists In Reconciliation

If the offender (Party B) still refuses to listen and understand and the relationship is not reconciled, the offended (Party A) asks representatives of church leadership (such as a pastor, Pastor Parish Relations, the Elders, or the Session) to meet with them for the explicit purpose of assisting with listening and understanding so the relationship can be reconciled.

5. When The Offender Is Unwilling To Be Reconciled,

the church is to regard the offender (Party B) as a *pagan or corrupt tax collector,* or one who has chosen to stand outside of the boundaries of belonging established by God and who has chosen to not be reconciled within the church. However, in treating Party B as one who has chosen to stand outside the boundaries of belonging, the church still continues to love and to seek restored relationship with the offender.

We must have a sea anchor, or relational covenant, to withstand and navigate the storms.

FINAL REMINDER: Every step in this divinely designed process which Jesus has established and taught us is for the explicit purpose of RECONCILIATION. Therefore, at no point should any of these steps or actions be used to "take sides" or to "get even." Only reconciled, healed, and restored relationships should be sought.

Casting the Anchor in Covenant

It is critically important for us to remember that STORMING, or conflict, is both natural and inevitable in any group. Additionally, STORMING is important in our process of discerning and following God's will. Conflict itself is not what harms us, but how we respond to the conflict can. Therefore, we must put into practice these essential biblical skills for healthy storming so we can navigate through the storms in a safe manner.

These skills and behaviors also become the basis for a relational covenant that will protect the integrity of WHO we are and WHOSE we are on this journey. The purpose of the relational covenant is to define how we choose to relate to one another as brothers and sisters in Christ and as co-ministers in our mission (see Appendix A for sample relational covenants).

Without a sea anchor, a boat can be severely tossed and torn in a storm and eventually destroyed. However, once the sea anchor is properly deployed, the boat is turned face on in the storm and can weather the storm safely. Without a relational covenant,

Before we can Norm, we must know how to Storm.

when our differing views, opinion, wishes, needs, and desires clash together, our relationships can also be tossed, torn, and even destroyed. However, with a relational covenant in place, we can safely approach our differences and difficulties straight on without fear of destruction.

God required clear relational boundaries in the form of a covenant among the Israelites on their journey of faith. After their release from bondage, but before entering into the Promised Land, God established a relational covenant with and among the people that clearly communicated Who they were and Whose they were in their life and journey together.

> *Then Moses went up to God, and the Lord called to him from the mountain and said, "This is what you are to say to the house of Jacob and what you are to tell the people of Israel: 'You yourselves have seen what I did to Egypt, and how I carried you on eagles' wings and brought you to myself. Now if you obey me fully and keep my covenant, then out of all nations you will be my treasured possession. Although the whole earth is mine, you will be for me a kingdom of priests and a holy nation.' These are the words you are to speak to the Israelites."*
>
> **Exodus 19:1-6 NIV**

In this context, the Lord established a relational covenant among the people that would protect the integrity of their relationships and the Promise set before them. Of course, we know this relational covenant as the Ten Commandments as found in Exodus 20. The first of these commandments protected the people's relationship with God, and the last protected their relationships with one another. God reminded them that the promises would be fulfilled if they lived within the bounds of this covenant. However, if they chose to live outside this covenant, they would threaten the integrity of both their relationships and the Promise.

The same is true for us today. Within the bounds of a biblical relational covenant, our relationships and God's promise for us will be protected. However, without these boundaries in place, we are at great risk of harming our relationship and our ministries in the face of any storms.

Passing Through the Storms

Of all the four stages of our life and ministry together, STORMING is where we most often get stuck. Unless we begin to respond to conflict in ways that strengthen our relationships and ministry together, we will continue to oscillate back and forth between FORMING and STORMING. Without the essential biblical skills and a relational covenant, when we are faced with conflict one or more of us often get tossed on the shore or we choose to step out of the stream altogether. And once one or more of us has left the group because of STORMING, we must go back to FORMING again.

Although the storms are important in our life and ministry, we are not called to stay there! We must be able to move safely through these storms to be able to say, "YES! This is what we are about," and to say, "No, this is not what we are about" as we clarify our mission and purpose. The storms are not to be avoided, just safely navigated. A relational covenant embracing biblical skills empowers us to do precisely this.

119

Questions for Discussion

1. How has fear of the unknown caused anxiety or conflict among us?

2. When have we convened the "Back to Egypt Committee?"

3. Utilizing the following lead, develop a bibical relational covenant: **As co-laborers for the Kingdom of God at [Our Church or Specific Ministry], we commit to relate to one another in the following manner to maintain the integrity of our relationships and ministry.**

The Right Next Step for Chapter Six

Assign members of the group to conduct a demographic survey of your surrounding area or the geographic area for which your ministry is intended. Additionally, set aside time to meet with individuals in your church or ministry as well as your neighbors (or those you believe you are to serve) to assess their needs. Bring those results to share the next time you gather.

There are many resources available for gathering demographic information. The US Census Bureau offers information for free. Local realtors may have local demographic information. Information is also available for purchase through companies that specialize in providing churches with this information, such as Percept.

Scripture & Prayers
Day 1
Exodus 33:12-14

Moses said to the Lord, "See, you have said to me, 'Bring up this people;' but you have not let me know whom you will send with me. Yet you have said, "I know you by name, and you have also found favor in my sight. Now if I have found favor in your sight, show me your ways, so that I may know you and find favor in your sight. Consider too that this nation is your people." He said, "My presence will go with you, and I will give you rest." NRSV

Lord, I know it was scary for Moses to lead the people into the wilderness. It is scary for me to be a Christian in today's world. Please give me the faith to walk with your Holy Spirit. I am strengthened for this journey and my fellow travelers are strengthened. You are wonderful. Thank you.

Focus Notes

Day 2
Matthew 16:21-22

From that time on Jesus began to explain to his disciples that he must go to Jerusalem and suffer many things...and that he must be killed and on the third day be raised to life. Peter took him aside and began to rebuke him, "Never, Lord!" he said. "This shall never happen to you!" NIV

Jesus, just as Peter feared the future and its unforeseen and unwanted circumstances and changes, so do we. We often rebuke you and each other with a "Never!" Help us remember to protect our relationships with you and one another by casting an anchor of trust in you and one another. Help us not fear the storms but to acknowledge them and face them so we will not be shipwrecked due to mutiny or indecision.

Day 3
Titus 3:1-2
Remind your people to obey the rulers and authorities and

Focus Notes

not to be rebellious. They must always be ready to do something helpful and not say cruel things or argue. They should be gentle and kind to everyone. CEV

Lord, only you can teach us true humility and submission. We are prone to rebellion and to seek control. Forgive us and make us more like you. Give us hearts of understanding and compassion. Help us seek good for others rather than just for ourselves. Teach us to be peacemakers for you said, "Blessed are the peacemakers for they shall be called children of God." We want to be known as your children and represent you faithfully and honorably.

Day 4
Matthew 12:34b
Your words show what is in your hearts. CEV

Lord Jesus, create in me a pure heart so I may not speak evil of your children. Remind me that my words are a reflection of what is in my heart. Let my speech pronounce blessing and not curses. Let me speak words that edify your Body, the Church. Help me always remember that when I speak of the Church, I am speaking of you and your Body.

Day 5
2 Corinthians 5:19-20
For God was in Christ, reconciling the world to himself, no longer counting people's sins against them. This is the wonderful message he has given us to tell others. We are Christ's ambassadors, and God is using us to speak to you. We urge you, as though Christ himself were here pleading with you, "Be reconciled to God!" NLT

Focus Notes

Almighty God, you are the Great Reconciler. You have also called us to be reconcilers. You have committed to us the same ministry as that of Jesus—to reconcile us to you and to each other. Help us not be agents of the enemy and cause division, but to be agents of Christ and pursue unity. Help us seek forgiveness in our relationships and not count each other's sins against them as you have not counted ours.

Only through true forgiveness can we minister together and release one another into ministry.

Day 6
Genesis 1:16
And the Lord God commanded the man, "You may freely eat of every tree of the garden; but of the tree of the knowledge of good and evil you shall not eat, for in the day that you eat of it you shall die." NRSV

Focus Notes

2 Corinthians 3:17
Now the Lord is the Spirit, and where the Spirit of the Lord is, there is freedom. NIV

Lord, you have given us boundaries from the beginning of creation. You have given us boundaries to protect us from the enemy and from one another. Teach us how to respect and acknowledge these limits so that we may live in harmony and in peace with one another. Let us be led by your Spirit within us and not by our own desires. You have given us great freedom and the keys to an infinite Kingdom. Help us remember that your Kingdom is boundless when we walk in obedience to you.

Day 7
Acts 27:17
Fearing that they would run aground in Syritis, they lowered the sea anchor and let the ship be driven along. NIV

Lord Jesus, help us

Trust in the Lord
with all your heart;
do not depend
on your own
understanding.
Seek his will
in all you do,
And he will direct
your paths.

Proverbs 3:5-6

Six

Define Mission / Vision
① who we are
② whose we are
③ what we called to Do

Hearing the Cries of the Needy

Once we cast the sea anchor that states WHO we are and WHOSE we are, we can begin to clarify WHAT God is calling us to do. Together, these three factors define our mission and vision around which we must NORM as a group. When we cast this second anchor and norm around a shared mission and vision, we can readily say "Yes" to what God is calling us to do, and we can with confidence say "No" to those things (even "good things") that are not consistent with our unique calling from God.

① *Needs around us*

So how do we now define our unique calling around which we must NORM? In the next three chapters, we will explore the dynamics of two aspects which define our mission and vision: the needs that surround us and our unique calling to respond to these needs.

② *Respond to needs*

We live in a broken and hurting world, and the love and grace of our Lord and Savior, Jesus Christ is this hurting world's only hope of restoration. There is a balm in Gilead, and his name is Jesus! Eventually, all of us can testify how we, too, have been healed and restored—spiritually, physically, or emotionally—through the love and grace of Jesus Christ. As ones who have been healed and redeemed, we are likewise called to be Christ's instruments of healing and redemption for this broken and hurting world.

Released to Release
By grace, we are healed and redeemed, and in response to this grace, we are to be instruments of healing and redemption. Out

CALLS us to Respond to Needs of the

of our own brokenness, God restores us and calls us to respond to the needs of others.

Throughout Scripture, we see this repeated pattern of God releasing to become instruments of release. Of these, the most striking may be Moses. Born a Hebrew slave, Moses was raised as an Egyptian prince. However, at his core Moses knew WHO he was and WHOSE he was as his identity was inherently bound to the suffering of the Israelites.

> *God heals and restores us to become instruments of healing and restoration for others.*

In fact, it was the sight of his people's suffering that triggered in Moses an uncontainable passion that led to murder.

Many years later, when Moses had grown up, he went out to visit his people, the Israelites, and he saw how hard they were forced to work. During his visit, he saw an Egyptian beating one of the Hebrew slaves. After looking around to make sure no one was watching, Moses killed the Egyptian and buried him in the sand.

Exodus 2:11-12 NLT

The next day, Moses was confronted with the act, and so he fled to the land of Midian. In God's mercy and timing, Moses was released from his failure and fear of being caught through the care of Jethro, the priest of Midian. Moses was released and nurtured for the ultimate purpose of becoming an instrument of God's release for the Israelites out of Egypt.

Like Moses, we, too, have been released from our failures and fear of the past through the redemptive grace of God.

HAYWOOD

Additionally, like Moses we have been released for the purpose
of being instruments of release for others from poverty, sickness,
oppression, and brokenness. To deny this call is to respond
ungraciously to this incredible gift of God's grace. On the
other hand, to accept our call to be vessels of God's healing
and restoration is our response-ability to God's healing and
restoration for us.

Cries Precede the Call

As we begin to tune into our unique calling from God, the
cries of the broken and hurting are some of the first voices
we must hear. When God called Moses to release his people
from bondage in Egypt, God did not begin by telling Moses
how perfect he was for the task. Instead, God began by
acknowledging the cries of his people.

> One day, Moses was taking care of the sheep and goats of his
> father-in-law Jethro, the priest of Midian, and Moses decid-
> ed to lead them across the desert to Sinai, the holy mountain.
> There an angel of the LORD appeared to him from a burn-
> ing bush. Moses saw that the bush was on fire, but it was
> not burning up. "This is strange!" he said to himself. "I'll go
> over and see why the bush isn't burning up." When the LORD
> saw Moses coming near the bush, he called him by name,
> and Moses answered, "Here I am." God replied, "Don't come
> any closer. Take off your sandals—the ground where you are
> standing is holy. I am the God who was worshiped by your
> ancestors Abraham, Isaac, and Jacob." Moses was afraid to
> look at God, and so he hid his face. The LORD said: I have seen
> how my people are suffering as slaves in Egypt, and I have
> heard them beg for my help because of the way they are being
> mistreated. I feel sorry for them, and I have come down to
> rescue them from the Egyptians. I will bring my people out of
> Egypt into a country where there is good land, rich with milk
> and honey. I will give them the land where the Canaanites,

Hittites, Amorites, Perizzites, Hivites, and Jebusites now live. My people have begged for my help, and I have seen how cruel the Egyptians are to them. Now go to the king! I am sending you to lead my people out of his country.

Exodus 3:1-10 CEV

Our call from God begins with the cries of others in need.

God had heard the cries of his people in Egypt, and in response to these cries, God called Moses. Moses' ministry was directly defined by the cries of those in need. When God called and sent out the prophets, it was always in response to the needs of God's people and what God needed to see changed in them.

Jesus, too, was sent by God to respond to the needs of this broken and hurting world. In the gospel of Luke, Jesus first declares publicly his call in relation to the needs of the people:

He went to Nazareth, where he had been brought up, and on the Sabbath day he went into the synagogue, as was his custom. And he stood up to read. The scroll of the prophet Isaiah was handed to him. Unrolling it, he found the place where it is written: "The Spirit of the Lord is on me,   because he has anointed me to preach good news to the poor. He has sent me to proclaim freedom for the prisoners and recovery of sight for the blind, to release the oppressed, to proclaim the year of the Lord's favor."

Luke 4:16-19 NIV

Jesus was sent to respond to the poor, the prisoners, the blind, and the oppressed. As the body of Christ, the Church, we have likewise been sent to respond to these needs in the world. In fact, Jesus tells us that we, the Church, will be finally judged on whether or not we responded to the cries of others around us:

> *But when the Son of Man comes in his glory, and all the angels with him, then he will sit upon his glorious throne. All the nations will be gathered in his presence, and he will separate them as a shepherd separates the sheep from the goats. He will place the sheep at his right hand and the goats at his left. Then the King will say to those on the right, 'Come, you who are blessed by my Father, inherit the Kingdom prepared for you from the foundation of the world. For I was hungry, and you fed me. I was thirsty, and you gave me a drink. I was a stranger, and you invited me into your home. I was naked, and you gave me clothing. I was sick, and you cared for me. I was in prison, and you visited me.' Then these righteous ones will reply, 'Lord, when did we ever see you hungry and feed you? Or thirsty and give you something to drink? Or a stranger and show you hospitality? Or naked and give you clothing? When did we ever see you sick or in prison, and visit you?' And the King will tell them, 'I assure you, when you did it to one of the least of these my brothers and sisters, you were doing it to me!'*

Matthew 25:31-40 NLT

Listening and responding faithfully to the cries of those around us largely determines obedience to our call. However, when we fail to listen to their needs, we often fall into the trap of doing what we choose instead of being a means of God's grace for others. Therefore, the first step in determining what God is calling us to do is to ask:

**Who are our neighbors,
And what do they need?**

Checking Out the Neighbors

The vision for ministry which God places before us is shaped by both our calling and our setting. Therefore, our particular

131

setting and circumstances greatly influence the way in which God chooses to use us to bring about his Kingdom in our midst. For example, our church may be located in a transitioning neighborhood with a growing international population. Or our congregation may have an elderly population with increasing needs for support services. When faced with these situations, we must grasp God's call to respond to the circumstances as opposed to fleeing from these needs to find other "neighbors."

> *To be obedient to God's call, we must respond to the needs*

Downtown Community [handwritten margin note]

When we ask the question, "Who are our neighbors?" we may wonder if we should look inside or outside our walls. The answer would be "Yes." God calls us to minister both within our church and out in the world since our "neighbors" exist in both places.

At the end of his earthly ministry before ascending to the Father, Jesus told his followers:

> **But you will receive power when the Holy Spirit has come upon you; and you will be my witnesses in Jerusalem, in all Judea and Samaria, and to the ends of the earth.**
>
> **Acts 1:8 NRSV**

Jesus was describing the ever-widening neighborhood in which he has called us to serve. We are sent to minister and give witness to the love of Jesus Christ within our own families, our churches, and our immediate neighborhoods. However, the widening circles do not end there. Jesus has also sent us to those neighbors and neighborhoods we would honestly rather ignore (the "Samaritans") and even to the people we've been taught to avoid (such as the Gentiles for ancient Jews).

Loving our neighbors has been inextricably tied with our obedience to God's will (see Luke 10:25-27). However, like the Jewish legal expert who questioned Jesus, we may struggle with understanding who is our neighbor. When asked this question, Jesus responded with a radical answer through the story of the Good Samaritan:

> *A Jewish man was traveling on a trip from Jerusalem to Jericho, and he was attacked by bandits. They stripped him of his clothes and money, beat him up, and left him half dead beside the road. By chance a Jewish priest came along; but when he saw the man lying there, he crossed to the other side of the road and passed him by. A Temple assistant walked over and looked at him lying there, but he also passed by on the other side. Then a despised Samaritan came along, and when he saw the man, he felt deep pity. Kneeling beside him, the Samaritan soothed his wounds with medicine and bandaged them. Then he put the man on his own donkey and took him to an inn, where he took care of him. The next day he handed the innkeeper two pieces of silver and told him to take care of the man. 'If his bill runs higher than that,' he said, 'I'll pay the difference the next time I am here.' "Now which of these three would you say was a neighbor to the man who was attacked by bandits?" Jesus asked. The man replied, "The one who showed him mercy." Then Jesus said, "Yes, now go and do the same."*

Luke 10:30-37 NLT

In his telling of the parable, Jesus unexpectedly turned the tables where the neighbor was not the one in need but rather the instrument of God's grace! Furthermore, the Samaritan was the least liked and the least likely, according to the Jews, to be chosen as the best "neighbor." However, Jesus was teaching us that to fulfill God's command to love our neighbor, we must be willing to serve anyone in need AND to be served by anyone who God sends—regardless of who they are or from whence they come.

Sometimes God calls us and sends us out to serve so we, too, can be "saved." How often have we returned from a mission trip with the realization that we were the ones whose lives had been changed?

When we ask the question, "Who are our neighbors?" we must make sure that our gaze is not too limited or lowered. Instead, we must actively look around us to find the least, the last, and the lost. And we must even acknowledge that in finding our neighbors, we might also discover that we might be the ones "found" and changed by them.

Changing Neighborhoods

We live in a rapidly changing world, and many of our churches find themselves surrounded by rapidly changing neighborhoods. As our neighbors change, their needs change as well. Therefore, it is not safe for us to assume that we automatically know specifically WHO our neighbors are or WHAT they need.

At least every five years, we should actively assess the demographics of our neighbors to determine WHO they are. Various online studies based on census data (such as Percept) provide a tremendous amount of information regarding the people who surround our churches and some initial insight regarding their needs.

Changing neighborhoods = Changing needs = Changing ministries.

Demographic studies and profiles provide very helpful information. However, the most effective assessment tool for knowing our neighbors is personally engaging them. The following are some practical ways in which we can learn who our neighbors are and seek to understand what they require:

- Walk through the neighborhood surrounding your church during the weekday or on a Sunday morning.
- Keep records of calls and requests for assistance that come to your church office or pastor.
- Attend community events for the explicit purpose of observing and listening to those present.
- Visit with local school officials and ask about the needs of students and their families.
- Meet with local government officials and ask what they see as needs in the community.
- Arrange a ride-along with the local law enforcement to understand the brokenness among your neighbors.

Assessing the Needs Holistically

As instruments of God's grace, we must also tend to the needs of others holistically. We must assess the spiritual, physical, and emotional needs of people and realize that we can not fairly respond to one particular aspect without addressing the other aspects as well.

Like Elisha, we must ask others, "What can we do to help you?"

For an un-churched homeless neighbor, his deep hunger for the Gospel of Jesus Christ will be satisfied once his belly is filled and his body clothed. To reflect the integrity of the Gospel, we can only offer him Christ once we have been the hands and feet of Christ to him first. Likewise, the family struggles we see prevalent in our neighborhoods may be reflective of the spiritual bankruptcy of their homes. Our call, then, is to assess and respond to the WHOLE lives of our neighbors. And in doing so, we must respond unabashedly in the name of Jesus who has sent us.

What Can We Do?

Dwelling with our neighbors is essential in determining their needs, but we must also remember to ask them directly, "What can we do to help you?" Elisha the prophet was a powerful man of God, and yet he did not assume to know how God was going to use him. Instead, Elisha's miraculous ministry often flowed from asking those he encountered, "What can I do to help you?" (2 Kings 4).

Even though Jesus had the knowledge of God and the need was usually apparent in front of him, he, too, often asked this critical question.

> *Then they came to Jericho. As Jesus and his disciples, together with a large crowd, were leaving the city, a blind man, Bartimaeus (that is, the Son of Timaeus), was sitting by the roadside begging. When he heard that it was Jesus of Nazareth, he began to shout, "Jesus, Son of David, have mercy on me!" Many rebuked him and told him to be quiet, but he shouted all the more, "Son of David, have mercy on me!" Jesus stopped and said, "Call him." So they called to the blind man, "Cheer up! On your feet! He's calling you." Throwing his cloak aside, he jumped to his feet and came to Jesus. "What do you want me to do for you?" Jesus asked him. The blind man said, "Rabbi, I want to see." "Go," said Jesus, "your faith has healed you." Immediately he received his sight and followed Jesus along the road.*
>
> **Mark 10:46-52** NIV

By asking others directly how we can serve them, we also

communicate a personal desire to be an instrument of God's healing. We connect the "us" to "them" in the context of relationship. Out of our relationship with our neighbors, ministries will emerge that truly reflect the love and grace of Jesus Christ.

God has redeemed and released us to be his instruments of redemption and release. Therefore, to fulfill God's will for us, as individuals and as a church, we must listen to the cries of those around us and respond in ways that reflect our relationship with Jesus Christ. Jesus offers to heal and restore us spiritually, physically, and emotionally. As ones who are healed and restored by grace, we are called and sent to heal and restore God's people as well.

Questions for Discussion

Utilizing the demographic data and interviews conducted, address the following questions:

1. Who are our neighbors?
2. How have our neighbors or neighborhoods changed?
3. What are their needs?
4. How are their needs currently being met?

The Right Next Step for Chapter Seven

In Chapter Seven, you will discover your Burning Bush by exploring your spiritual gifts, your passion, and your joy for ministry.

Choose a spiritual gift inventory to be used by all the members of your group (or even the congregation.) Distribute copies of the inventory to all members and have them complete the inventory and bring it to your next session. Remember to use one common inventory of the group or leadership's choosing so the results and terminology will be comparable. Compile the group's results to identify the 3-5 most prevalent spiritual gifts among the group.

Note: Further discussion of spiritual gifts and resources is available in Appendix B.

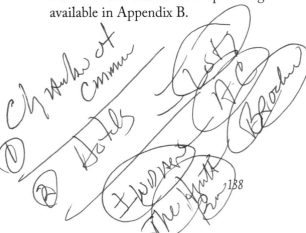

Scripture & Prayers
Day 1
2 Corinthians 1:3-4

All praise to the God and Father of our Lord Jesus Christ. He is the source of every mercy and the God who comforts us. He comforts us in all our troubles so that we can comfort others. When others are troubled, we will be able to give them the same comfort God has given us. CEV

God we do praise you as the God of all comfort and compassion. You have been our comfort in times of trouble not just for our sake but also for the sake of others. Help us respond to those in pain with the same comfort we have received. One of the greatest gifts we can give is the gift of mercy and compassion. Help us remember that it is our calling and our command to do so as your disciples here on earth.

Focus Notes

Day 2
Acts 9:15-18

But the Lord said to him, "Go, for he is an instrument whom I have chosen to bring my name before Gentiles and kings and before the people of Israel; I myself will show him how much he must suffer for the sake of my name." So Ananias went and entered the house. He laid his hands on Saul and said, "Brother Saul, the Lord Jesus, who appeared to you on your way here, has sent me so that you may regain your sight and be filled with the Holy Spirit." And immediately something like scales fell from his eyes, and his sight was restored. Then he got up and was baptized. NRSV

Jesus, thank you for using someone like Saul to teach us about grace and release. He was released from a life of deep sin and evil in order to be an instrument of release for others. Thank you that we are not called in our perfection and strength but in our weakness and sin. Teach us all to be instruments of release and restoration to others, even to those whom we have bound or broken.

Focus Notes

Day 3
Judges 3:9,15; 6:7
But when they cried out to the Lord, he raised up for them a deliverer. Again the Israelites cried out to the Lord, and he gave them a deliverer. When the Israelites cried to the Lord because of Midain, he sent them a prophet. NIV

Matthew 25:40
And the king will answer them, "Truly I tell you, just as you did it to one of the least of these who are members of my family, you did it to me." NRSV

Gracious God, you hear our cries and you meet our needs. You hear our audible cries and the cries of our hearts. Teach us to hear those around and us and not be blind or deaf to their needs. Help us remember that

the cries come from those you call your children. When we touch them, we touch you, and when we ignore them, we ignore you. Let us not pass you by.

Day 4

Mark 12:28-31

One of the teachers of the Law… asked him, "Of all the commandments, which is most important?" "The most important one," answered Jesus, "is this: 'Hear, O Israel, the Lord God, the Lord, is one. Love the Lord with all your heart, and with all your soul, and will all your mind and all your strength.' The second is this, love your neighbor as yourself." NIV

Jesus, you not only ask us to love our neighbor, but you command it. You also tell us the only thing greater is love of God. Impress upon us the magnitude of this, Jesus. Help us to remember that this is the only other reason we are here other than to worship and glorify you. It is in fact part of our worship as we walk in obedience to you and your desires. As James said, "No one has ever seen God, but if we love another, then God's love is made complete is us."

> **Focus Notes**

Day 5
James 2:1-2
My dear brothers and sisters, how can you claim that you have faith in our glorious Lord Jesus Christ if you favor some people more than others? For instance, suppose someone comes into your meeting dressed in fancy clothes and expensive jewelry, and another comes in who is poor and dressed in shabby clothes. NLT

Focus Notes

Lord, let us remember that we tend to judge and favor one person over another and one group over another. Our neighbors are not always those whom we would choose and our neighborhoods are not always what we would choose, but it is where you have placed us. Give us spiritual eyes to love all equally and to accept all regardless of place or position. You have called us to love our neighbors. Give us the grace to be loving.

Day 6
John 4:5-7
So he came to a town in Samaria called Sychar, near the plot of ground Jacob had given to his son Joseph. Jacob's well was there, and Jesus, tired as he was from the journey, sat down by the well. It was about the sixth hour. When a Samaritan woman came to

draw water, Jesus said to her, "Will you give me a drink?" NIV

Jesus, you know what we really need. You place us in circumstances that will minister to us and where we can minister to others. Help us balance the two. Help us to minister and be ministered to. Help us to stop at the well and drink of your grace and to offer a drink to others as well. You are the God of Grace. Allow us the refreshing gift of that grace and encourage us to share your grace that is so freely shared with us.

Day 7
John 13:14-15
So if I, your Lord and
Teacher, have washed your
feet, you also ought to wash
one another's feet.

For I have set you an
example, that you also
should do as I have done to
you. NRSV

*We want to follow that
example, Jesus. We want to
be able to bow in humility
to serve and be served. Help
and teach us how to wash one*
another's feet, our neighbor's feet, and to let them wash ours. Give us the grace and humility of a little child. Teach us that humility and service are the true marks of your disciples. Give us joy in serving you and joy in serving each other.

Focus Notes

Trust in the Lord
with all your heart;
do not depend
on your own
understanding.
Seek his will
in all you do,
And he will direct
your paths.

Proverbs 3:5-6

Seven

Finding Our Burning Bush

Once we begin listening to the cries of those around us, we often become overwhelmed with a deluge of needs. Obviously, each church does not have the resources (personal, spiritual, or financial) to respond to all the needs of our neighbors. However, every individual and every church has the ability to respond in some particular way. Discerning our call involves finding where the needs of our neighbors intersect with our unique ability to respond.

Needs of Our Neighbors

Our Unique Ability to Respond

In addition to being overwhelmed with the needs, we also may wonder what difference one person—or one church—can make. Of course, there are plenty examples of remarkable individuals and remarkable churches making a world of difference. And in

145

those cases, it's easy enough to see their call to serve this broken and hurting world. But for many of us, we may question if and how God can use us, and as a result, we expect someone else "more able" to respond to God's call.

One in Ministry to All the World

The call to minister to the needs of this world could never be fulfilled by any individual or any one church. Instead, this grand calling requires the response of all of us as believers doing our own particular part.

Every member, every church, is uniquely called as an instrument of God's healing and grace.

Just as our bodies have many parts and each part has a special function, so it is with Christ's body. We are all parts of his one body, and each of us has different work to do. And since we are all one body in Christ, we belong to each other, and each of us needs all the others.
Romans 12:4-5 NLT

All of us together in a local congregation are one body, and all churches together form the One Body of Christ. In the same way a human body requires all the individual parts to function as God designed them, the Body of Christ requires that all members and all churches function as God uniquely designed us as well.

In the Body of Christ, every member and every church are necessary to respond adequately to God's call for us to be instruments of healing for this broken and hurting world. Therefore, we should not argue that we have no part to play because we can't do "this" or we aren't members "there." To this excuse, the apostle Paul responds:

Indeed, the body does not consist of one member but of many. If the foot would say, "Because I am not a hand, I do not be-

long to the body," that would not make it any less a part of the body. And if the ear would say, "Because I am not an eye, I do not belong to the body," that would not make it any less a part of the body. If the whole body were an eye, where would the hearing be? If the whole body were hearing, where would the sense of smell be? But as it is, God arranged the members in the body, each one of them, as he chose. If all were a single member, where would the body be? As it is, there are many members, yet one body. The eye cannot say to the hand, "I have no need of you," nor again the head to the feet, "I have no need of you." On the contrary, the members of the body that seem to be weaker are indispensable,

1 Corinthians 12:14-21 NRSV

Every individual, every church, must do their own unique part in the Body of Christ for us to reflect Christ adequately for this world. No church is too small. No person is insignificant.

> *In fact, some of the parts that seem weakest and least important are really the most necessary.*

1 Corinthians 12:22 NLT

The question, then, is not IF we are called but rather How God is uniquely calling us to respond.

Throughout Scripture, we hear examples of God calling forth individuals to respond to the needs of his people and his world. God called Noah to build a big boat to save a vestige of humanity from the world's flood of evil. God called Abram to leave a land he loved and to the seemingly impossible task of fathering a nation. God called Moses to free the Israelites from Egypt and Deborah to lead the people

The question is not IF we are called, but How God is calling us.

into battle. God called David to rule, Esther to intercede, Peter to preach, and Paul to plant.

From the beginning of time to the present age, God has called people to minister for the sake of his Kingdom. However, a closer look at many of these individuals reveals a broader call of God for a group or team of individuals. Along with Noah, God called his family. Beside Abram was Sarai. Moses had Miriam and Aaron. Jonathan supported David. Mordecai assisted Esther. Even Jesus employed the twelve, and Paul teamed with Barnabas, Silas, Priscilla, and many others. Furthermore, there were the innumerable unnamed persons behind the scenes whose stories we do not know but whose obedience to God's call ultimately changed our lives.

Each of these faithful servants did their own unique part in unfolding God's plan for the restoration of his world. And of course, the unfolding did not stop with them. God's call is as real and critical today as it ever has been. As the cries of the needy grow louder, God's call on our lives grows stronger. As long as there is a need, there will be a call. Therefore we must discover what God is uniquely calling us to do.

Function Flows from Identity

WHAT God calls us to Do will always be consistent with WHO God has created us to BE. In other words, our function, or what we do for God, should flow from our true identity that comes from God. However, too often in our lives and even in our ministries, the process goes more like this: "Because I have been prepared 'this' way, I must function like 'this.' And since 'this' is my function, "this" must be my identity."

Preparation

Function

Identity

This particular approach to understanding our calling, however, presents several problems. First, when we allow our human-gained preparation to define exclusively our function, then what we do for God is based more on our own strength and abilities and relies less on the strength and abilities that God will give us. Secondly, our preparation might also be more directly shaped by the expectations and parameters of the world than by God, and thus our function and identity will be shaped by the world as well. When this happens, we may find ourselves conflicted between fulfilling what the world wants us to do and what God wants us to do. In many ways, this describes the crisis of identity and function in which many individuals and churches find themselves today.

By contrast, when we commit ourselves to *stepping in the stream of God's will*, we look first and foremost to defining WHO we are and WHOSE we are in God. Since we truly believe that each of us has a particular part in the unfolding of God's plan to restore the world back to relationship with God, we must trust that God has designed each of us with this plan in mind.

> *You made all the delicate, inner parts of my body and knit me together in my mother's womb. Thank you for making me so wonderfully complex! Your workmanship is marvelous—and how well I know it. You watched me as I was being formed in utter seclusion, as I was woven together in the darkness of the womb. You saw me before I was born. Every day of my life was recorded in your book. Every moment was laid out before a single day had passed.*
>
> **Psalm 139:13-16 NLT**

> *The word of the Lord came to me, saying, "Before I formed you in the womb I knew you, before you were born I set you apart; I appointed you as a prophet to the nations."*
>
> **Jeremiah 1:4-5 NIV**

Who God has created us to be will define What God has called us to do. And once we discern the nature of our calling, we will understand more clearly how we need to be prepared.

Many of us have heard the saying: **"God does not call the equipped. God equips the called."** Undoubtedly, God uses our life experiences and educational preparation to fulfill His will in us and through us. However, when we look first to God to define our call, then our preparation results from obedience to the call instead of our function being dictated by any confines of our preparation.

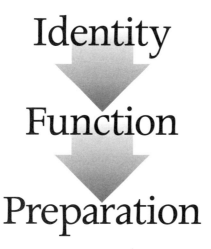

Identity

Function

Preparation

Calling from the Core

Our calling will emerge from the nature of our being and our being in relationship with others. God has created each of us with specific gifts and abilities that are to be used in the context of our relationships. Moses is a good example.

Moses was born as a Hebrew slave, and yet he was raised as an Egyptian prince. As a boy and young man, he belonged to Egypt, but his true heart belonged to God.

> *Then after Moses grew up, his faith made him refuse to be called Pharaoh's grandson. He chose to be mistreated with God's people instead of having the good time that sin could bring for a little while. Moses knew that the treasures of Egypt were not as wonderful as what he would receive from suffering for the Messiah, and he looked forward to his reward.*
>
> **Hebrews 11:24-26 CEV**

What an incredible statement of faith regarding the identity of Moses! The writer of Hebrews tells us that Moses forsook the worldly promises his identity with Egypt would provide to identify himself with a yet unknown Messiah and his suffering. Somewhere deep at his core, Moses knew he belonged to God and to the people of God, and Moses knew that God was calling him out to serve them.

God uses the ordinary in extraordinary ways to get our attention.

When Moses stepped out in faith to claim the core of WHO and WHOSE he was, Moses' function also started to change. As an Egyptian prince, Moses had everything done for him, but once he fled from Egypt, he became a shepherd—the very idenity and function the Egyptians despised! As a shepherd and nomad, no longer defined by the comforts and confines of a palace, Moses' leadership and passion for God's people were being honed to prepare him to be a shepherd-leader for the Israelites. Moses, however, did not understand the manifestation of this calling until he encountered the burning bush.

The Burning Bush

As we discussed in Chapter Six, God called Moses from a burning bush in response to the cries of the Israelites (Exodus 3:1-4:17). Most of us would agree that we don't expect God to call us from the middle of a blazing shrub. However, God often does use ordinary things in extraordinary ways for the purpose of getting our attention. A rainbow. A sling shot and five smooth stones. A tiny baby. Water. Bread and wine. With Moses, God used common fire and a bush, and yet the bush was not consumed, and it did get Moses' attention.

Even though we may not want God calling us from an actual burning bush, maybe there is something truly extraordinary about the ordinary occurrence of fire.

For many years, we have understood that three elements are necessary for a fire to start and to keep burning:
1. Fuel, or combustible material that will burn
2. Heat, or the energy needed for ignition to occur
3. Oxygen, at least 16% present in the atmosphere, such as air.

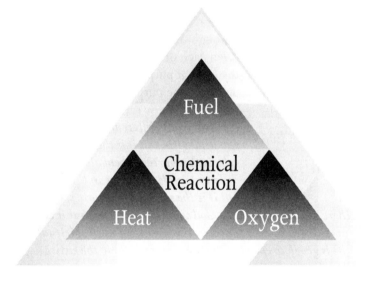

To have a fire, all three of these elements must be present together. However, recently we have also discovered that a fourth condition must be present:
4. Chemical reaction.

We now know that a chemical reaction, or sequence of events, must occur when the fuel, heat, and oxygen come together at just the right time, under just the right circumstances. Thus what was previously called the fire triangle is now known as the fire tetrahedron.

In much the same way, our call to ministry, or BURNING BUSH, is finding the intersection of four things:
1. Our spiritual gifts
2. Our passion for ministry
3. Our joy in service
4. The fullness of God's timing and circumstances.

Our Spiritual Gifts

Every member is gifted by the Holy Spirit to fulfill the functions of the Body of Christ.

Through the Holy Spirit, God has given each of us specific abilities for the explicit purpose to serve God. Paul describes the purpose of these special abilities when he says:

Now there are different kinds of spiritual gifts, but it is the Holy Spirit who is the source of them all. There are different kinds of service in the church, but it is the same Lord we are serving. There are different ways God works in our lives, but it is the same God who does the work through all of us. A spiritual gift is given to each of us as a means of helping the entire church.

1 Corinthians 12:4-7 NLT

As baptized believers, we are all gifted by the Holy Spirit for the purpose of carrying out the service or calling of the Church. There are many different gifts, and many people have more than one gift. However, no gift is greater or more important than any other, and all the gifts are to be used to serve God in the context of the Church.

In his letters to the churches, Paul describes many different spiritual gifts, and yet no list is comprehensive (see Romans 12:1-8, 1 Corinthians 12:1-31, and Ephesians 4:1-16). Spiritual gifts can basically be grouped into three categories. Gifts of **word** (or what we say) may include the gifts of apostleship, evangelism, prophecy, pastoring, teaching, encouragement, knowledge, and wisdom. Gifts of **deed** (or what we do) may include the gifts of assisting, giving, leadership, administration, compassion, faith, helps, mercy, and hospitality. The gifts of **sign** (or that which points to God) may include discernment, miracles, healing, tongues, interpretation, intercessory prayer, or spirit-music.

All of these gifts are essential and useful in the work of the church and in our service to the world. We cannot gain or get certain gifts since all spiritual gifts are given by God. Furthermore, all gifts are only useful if they are faithfully used.

> *God has also given each of us different gifts to use. If we can prophesy, we should do it according to the amount of faith we have. If we can serve others, we should serve. If we can teach, we should teach. If we can encourage others, we should encourage them. If we can give, we should be generous. If we are leaders, we should do our best. If we are good to others, we should do it cheerfully.*
>
> **Romans 12:6-8** CEV

With all members doing their own special part according to their God-given gifts and abilities, the Church will grow and function as the whole Body of Christ with Jesus as our Head (Ephesians 4:15-16). However, if all of us are not willing to claim and employ our gifts in service for God, then some members of the Body will be underused while others are at risk of being misused or abused.

Over the past several years, various resources have produced spiritual gift inventories to help individuals assess their own spiritual gifts. Whereas different inventories list different gifts of the Spirit, the primary purpose of all inventories is to clarify how we have been uniquely gifted by God to serve within the Church for the sake of his Kingdom (see Appendix B).

Our Passion for Ministry

Every fire requires enough heat for ignition, and every BURNING BUSH, or call to ministry, requires enough passion to set it aflame. Our passion for ministry is the spark that ignites us. Some may say it is what "trips their trigger." Passion is the emotion or the energy that is needed to get us and keep us going in ministry. The prophet Jeremiah described his passion when he said:

> *My heart, my heart—I writhe in pain! My heart pounds within me! I cannot be still.*
>
> **Jeremiah 4:19 NLT**

Jeremiah had a deep love for the people of God, and their wayward actions broke his heart. Throughout his ministry, Jeremiah's passion was often expressed as grief—a godly grief over the destruction of God's people that was a result of their sin.

> *O my Comforter in sorrow, my heart is faint within me. Listen to the cry of my people from a land far away: "Is the LORD not in Zion? Is her King no longer there?" "Why have they provoked me to anger with their images, with their worthless foreign idols?" "The harvest is past, the summer has ended, and we are not saved." Since my people are crushed, I am crushed; I mourn, and horror grips me. Is there no balm in Gilead? Is there no physician there? Why then is there no healing for the wound of my people?*
>
> **Jeremiah 8:18-22 NIV**

As Jeremiah witnessed the people around him dying and decaying in their own sin, he experienced deep emotions that sparked great energy which turned his passion into action:

I can't stop! If I say I'll never mention the LORD or speak his name, his word burns in my heart like a fire. It's like a fire in my bones! I am weary of holding it in!

Jeremiah 20:9 NLT

As we listen with heart to the cries of the needy, God's passion will become our passion. And yet God puts different passions within us. Some of us have a passion for helping the young, others for helping the aged. Some of us have a deep desire to bring health to the sick or to bring lost souls home to Jesus Christ.

Without passion, our ministry has no energy. Without emotion, our song of service is flat. But like Jeremiah, when our passion ignites our burning bush, we don't grow weary of doing something about it, but rather we grow weary of holding it in!

Our Joy in Service

What an amazing revelation that God desires us to actually enjoy our service. Our joy in service is our breath—our air—our *ruach*. The Hebrew word for breath or air is *ruach*, or the same word for Spirit. When we find the Holy Spirit breathing into our work, we are filled with new breath—new life—that is manifested in joy. Even in the most discouraging of circumstances, Nehemiah reminded the people:

The joy of the LORD is your strength!

Nehemiah 8:10 NLT

Unfortunately, joy is not always the primary motivator in our ministries. Too often, we are driven to serve out of obligation or guilt, but not joy. However, without joy, without the breath or Spirit within our ministries, like a fire without air, we will burn out.

When God called Ezekiel to minister to the Jews in captivity, Ezekiel was limited in what he could do without the work of the Holy Spirit in his midst. Ezekiel obediently did what God asked him to do as he called the dry bones together. But without the breath of God, Ezekiel's work had no life. So God said to Ezekiel:

> **Speak to the winds and say: "This is what the Sovereign LORD says: 'Come, O breath, from the four winds! Breathe into these dead bodies so that they may live again...' I will put my Spirit in you, and you will live."**
>
> **Ezekiel 37:9 & 14 NLT**

Without the Spirit in our work and true joy in our ministry, we often end up like those dry bones: lifeless and breathless. But when we minister out of joy, the Spirit flows freely, and our ministries will live again.

A body without breath is a dead body. Ministry without joy is a dead ministry.

Our joy in service, however, does not always mean being happy in our ministry. Happiness is contingent on external circumstances, but joy comes from deep within. While writing from prison to the church at Philippi, Paul repeatedly spoke of his joy:

> **But even if my life is to be poured out like a drink offering to complete the sacrifice of your faithful service (that is, if I am to die for you), I will rejoice, and I want to share my joy with all of you.**
>
> **Philippians 2:17 NLT**

Even in the face of death, Paul knew his joy in serving Christ and the Church. Therefore, nothing, not even chains, could contain his joy. The joy of the Lord was truly Paul's strength. Like Paul, when we minister in ways that bring us true joy, we and our ministries will experience new life, even in the face of death.

Fullness of God's Timing and Circumstances

The final aspect that must be present for our BURNING BUSH to be set ablaze is the fullness of God's timing and circumstances. There are times and places when our gifts, our passion, and even our joy seem to come together, and yet the calling is not yet clear.

Remember: our call to ministry is defined by both the circumstances or needs that surround us and our unique ability to respond. Therefore, our burning bush will always be made manifest in the context of these needs.

God had been developing the gifts and the passion in Moses for years before God called him from the burning bush. In Exodus 2:23, we hear that *years had passed* and the cries of people continued before God sent Moses to deliver them. The Israelites waited a long time for release. Moses may have even wondered if his life was being wasted. But in the fullness of God's timing and under just the right circumstances, God called Moses. Moses was "ready" to respond (at least ready for God's next season of preparation!), the Israelites were ready to accept Moses' message (although they still struggled with obeying it!), and Pharaoh's heart was being readied to rebel.

We can assess our spiritual gifts. We can identify our passions. We can even begin to articulate what gives us true joy. However, we cannot know the fullness of God's timing nor the circumstances in which God is going to act.

> *So when they had come together, they asked him, "Lord, is this the time when you will restore the kingdom to Israel?" He replied, "It is not for you to know the times or periods that the Father has set by his own authority.*
> **Acts 1:6-7 NRSV**

The prophet Habakkuk saw the plight of God's people and even sensed his call to respond. However, when he asked God how long he would have to wait for action, God told him:

> *These things I plan won't happen right away. Slowly, steadily, surely, the time approaches when the vision will be fulfilled. If it seems slow, wait patiently, for it will surely take place. It will not be delayed.*

Habakkuk 2:3 NLT

Finding the Intersection

God's vision for our lives and our ministries is revealed to us in the fullness of God's timing—not our own. Slowly, steadily, surely, the vision is revealed and ultimately fulfilled. Our responsibility is not to determine the timing. Ours is to find the intersection of the world's needs and our unique ability to respond.

As each of us individually finds and claims our BURNING BUSH, slowly, steadily, but surely the church's vision comes into focus as we begin to see clearly how God is calling us to respond. Individually, we discover our BURNING BUSH and then collectively our BURNING BUSHES become a spreading wildfire! As a group or church, we begin to see how our collective BURNING BUSHES define God's unique calling for us. With time, patience, and prayer, our vision for ministry will take place if we will faithfully pursue discerning that call. And no matter how long it takes, it will not be delayed.

Questions for Discussion

Collect and compile the spiritual gift inventory results of the group and /or congregation.

1. What are our most prevalant spiritual gifts?

2. What passions do we have for ministry? What excites us? What grieves us?

3. Where have we found the greatest joy—or new life—in serving others?

Note: Make a chart recording your gifts, passions, and joys in ministry. Also note any unique or particular circumstances, setting, or timing in which you find these aspects coming together.

The Right Next Step for Chapter Eight

Now that you are gaining clarity on your Burning Bush, you need to find the intersection of where the needs of your neighbors intersect with your unique ability or call to resond.

Make a chart comparing your neighbor's needs and aspects of your Burning Bush to find the intersection that will define God's unique vision for your ministry.

In Chapter Eight, you will begin to clarify God's unique calling or vision for your ministry.

Note: A chart or table to assist you in finding this intersection is available at www.steppinginthestream.org.

Scripture & Prayers
Day 1
Exodus 2:11 - 13

After Moses had grown up he went out to where his own people were and watched them at hard labor. The next day, he went out and saw two Hebrews fighting. He asked the one in the wrong, "Why are you hitting your fellow Hebrew?" NIV

God of grace and power, You created us with a sense and essence of who we are, whose we are, and where we came from. At our core we are yours, but we still have another identity while we are here. You placed that there also. Help us remember it is for bringing your Kingdom to earth and for carrying out your plans for us and for your people.

┌─────────────────────┐
│   **Focus Notes** │
│   │
│   │
│   │
│   │
│   │
└─────────────────────┘

Day 2
Exodus 3:11

But Moses said to God, "Who am I, that I should go to Pharaoh and bring the Israelites out of Egypt?" NIV

Lord, help us not fear the bush that burns before us. You have put it there to bring us to you. You have also put it there to bring others to you and to deliver them from their oppressors. When we approach this fire we are at the heart and essence and our being. We stand naked before you, not just barefoot, but exposed. Help us remember that we are covered by your wings of protection and robes of righteousness. Like Joseph's coat of many colors signified his kingship, your robes and your wings signify our belonging and protection. No weapon forged against us shall prosper.

Day 3
Exodus 2:19
They answered, "An Egyptian rescued us from the shepherds. He even drew water for us and watered the flock." NIV

Exodus 3:1
Now Moses was tending the flock of Jethro, his father in law, the priest of Midian, and he led the flock to the far side of the desert. NIV

Focus Notes

Jesus, like you, Moses' people did not even recognize him at first, but they recognized his servant nature and humility. He was prepared to lead and to serve through his daily service as a shepherd. He first led a flock to the far side of the desert but he later led a people. Help us to know Jesus, that you are using us everyday for your Kingdom. You are preparing us for greater works.

Day 4
3 John:3
I have no greater joy than to hear my children are walking in the Truth. NIV

Psalm 45:7
You love what is right and hate what is wrong. Therefore God, your God, has anointed you, pouring out the oil of joy on you more than on anyone else. NLT

Jesus, you were known for your joy. Our gifts, our calling, our countenance should express joy when we are walking in your will and in your gifting. Our greatest joy is experienced when we are operating in our gifting and under your anointing. Our greatest joy should be to see your children coming to know you and worship you, no matter if we are in the ministry or the marketplace. Help us know what true joy is and know the true joy of serving you with passion and with zeal.

Day 5
Psalm 69:9
My love for your house burns in me like a fire. CEV

John 2:17
The disciples then remembered that the Scriptures say, "My love for your house burns in me like a fire." CEV

> ## Focus Notes

Jesus, you were a man of passion. You were on fire with concern for what was important to you. Let our hearts burn for the things you have set before us and within us to accomplish your good works. Help us recognize the passion you have given us. Help us to embrace it as you did. It is the heat that keeps the fire for your Kingdom burning. You gave us passion and zeal to do your holy purposes. Teach us to recognize the fire burning within us for you and your house.

Day 6
Matthew 9:36
When he saw the crowds, he had compassion for them, because they were harassed and helpless, like sheep without a shepherd. NRSV

Focus Notes

Jesus, you encountered the helpless and the needy at every turn. We also encounter those who are in need. Help us know when it is our place and in our gifting and calling to help. Even you passed by many. Give us peace to let go, but give us strength to take hold of what you call us to. Help us learn to know when our calling and the need intersect. Help us also remember that there are others with different gifts and passions to fill those gaps. You have provided for all.

Day 7
Mark 1:15-17
One day as Jesus was walking along the shores of the Sea of Galilee, he saw

Simon and his brother, Andrew, fishing with a net, for they were commercial fishermen. Jesus called out to them, "Come, be my disciples, and I will show you how to fish for people!" CEV

Jesus, you call us from our ordinary lives and our ordinary tasks to be coworkers in your Kingdom. You equip us daily, and you call us from where we are and who we are. Help us and teach us to understand this concept. Teach us to understand the joy set before us and the passion that should consume us. Let our "doing" flow like a river from our "being." Help us see the shape of the vessel that you have designed, and help us

Trust in the Lord
with all your heart;
do not depend
on your own
understanding.
Seek his will
in all you do,
And he will direct
your paths.

Proverbs 3:5-6

Eight

Casting the Anchor

God wants us to know the heavenly will and purpose for our lives and our ministries. And to make sure we understand that purpose, God gives us a clear picture of the preferable future and imparts to us a vision around which we can rally. God paints for us a picture of hope that is cast before us as a sure and steady anchor for our storm-tossed souls. (See Hebrews 6:18-19.)

Throughout human history, God has cast visions to motivate, guide, and move people along their journey of faith and to bring about God's Kingdom here on earth. For the Israelites, God painted a picture of the Promised Land. Through the prophet Isaiah, God painted a promise of the future glory of Jerusalem for those returning from exile. Through his teachings, Jesus painted a picture of the Kingdom of Heaven so others could choose to follow. Through the words of Paul, God painted a picture of the Day of Resurrection to promise life to those who daily faced death. And in the midst of exile and widespread persecution of believers, God gave to the apostle John a clear picture of a preferable future which moves and motivates us as believers today.

> *I saw a new heaven and a new earth. The first heaven and the first earth had disappeared, and so had the sea. Then I saw New Jerusalem, that holy city, coming down from God in heaven. It was like a bride dressed in her wedding gown and ready to meet her husband. I heard a loud voice shout from the throne: God's home is now with his people. He will live with them, and they will be his own. Yes, God will make his home among his people. He will wipe all tears from their*

eyes, and there will be no more death, suffering, crying, or pain. These things of the past are gone forever. Then the one sitting on the throne said: I am making everything new. Write down what I have said. My words are true and can be trusted. Everything is finished! I am Alpha and Omega, the beginning and the end. I will freely give water from the life-giving fountain to everyone who is thirsty. All who win the victory will be given these blessings. I will be their God, and they will be my people.

Revelation 21:1-7 CEV

From the scriptural gallery of God's paintings of the Promise, this vision of the new heaven and new earth may be the one that motivates and moves us the most: a time and a place where there is no more pain, no more suffering, where all of God's formerly broken children are restored into a whole and complete relationship with God through Jesus.

God's vision for us will be the unique part we are to play as instruments of God's healing.

This picture of our preferable future is the ultimate destination on our journey of faith. However, during the course of this study, we have also learned that even though the Kingdom is our ultimate destination, the journey toward that destination is what we are called to complete. In an awesome and even baffling way, God has called us to bring about this ultimate vision. As ones who are healed and restored through the love of Jesus Christ, we are called to bring about God's Kingdom one life, one day at a time here on earth. And we fulfill this calling by being instruments of healing for this broken and hurting world through which we journey.

To fulfill this ultimate Vision where there is no more pain or suffering, God imparts to us specific and unique ways we are called to be instruments of healing. God has for each of us, as individuals and as churches, a vision that will move us, motivate us, and guide us to say, "Yes!" to what God is uniquely calling us to do.

Why Not Just Do It?

In our performance-driven society, we may wonder why God doesn't simply tell us what to do so we can just do it! After all, why do we need a vision? Isn't the work itself, the PERFORMING, enough to bring us together to get the work done?

God gives us a vision to keep us on course, to clarify what we are about, and to remind us what we are not about. Without a clearly articulated vision, we can spend all of our resources doing good things but never accomplish the God-things that God has uniquely called us to do. Furthermore, without discerning God's vision, what we do becomes all about us, and our ministry lasts only as long as we do.

Great ministries are based on a great vision—not just a great leader.

Great ministries and great movements are always led by a God-given vision. And God-given visions rarely, if ever, die when an individual leader does. Dr. Martin Luther King, Jr., faithful believer and leader in the Civil Rights Movement, beautifully articulated God's vision for a preferable future when he said, "I have a dream." That dream, so powerfully presented that day on the National Mall, became the dream of untold numbers of people.

He gave the nation and the Civil Rights Movement a vision with words that have been quoted untold times since then. "I have a dream that one day this nation will rise up and live out the true meaning of its creed: 'We hold these truths to be self evident, that all men are created equal....'" "I have a dream that one day every valley shall be exalted, every hill and mountain shall be made low, and rough places will be made plains, and the crooked places will be made straight, and the glory of the Lord shall be revealed, and all flesh shall see it together."

By giving us his words, historic words, and words of Scripture tied together, King painted a picture of a preferable future so we could faithfully live into this new vision. This vision of a broken society being woven and knitted back together was what motivated and guided Dr. King. And even though Dr. King's leadership was priceless and powerful among the people, when he tragically died at the hands of man, the movement did not. Why? Because the people had coalesced not simply around a man but rather a vision that still motivates and moves many of us even today.

God's vision for us is crucial to both set the course and keep us on it—especially when the road gets rough. God's vision keeps us true to our purpose for bringing about the Kingdom.

Focus the Vision

As we have discussed in the previous two chapters, God's vision is defined by finding the intersection of the needs around us and our unique ability to respond to those needs. God's vision for us is specific to WHO God has created us to be and WHAT God has gifted us to do. Furthermore, we have discovered that the vision will be revealed in the context of our particular circumstances and in the fullness of God's timing. George Barna explains the importance of timing in the revelation of God's vision when he says:

"Vision comes when God determines you are ready to handle it. When the time is right, God will unveil the vision and will enable you to comprehend the vision. Your ability to grasp the vision is not a matter of human competence, but of spiritual preparation and a wholehearted yearning to obey the vision, no matter what the cost. Only God knows when we are truly ready for the vision, for it will radically reshape every aspect of our lives, and it will have a special purpose." (*Turning Vision into Action*, 37)

God's vision for us will be the unique and specific intersection of the needs of our neighbors and our BURNING BUSH or call to respond in a particular setting at a particular time. However, over time, all of these factors can change. Our neighbors change, our gifts, passion, and our joy may change, and our setting and circumstances change. Therefore, we must continually assess all the factors that define our vision to ensure that the vision is clearly in focus.

Vision = clear picture of a preferable future for brokenness we are sent to serve.

God's vision will be a clear picture of a preferable future for the broken and hurting world we have been sent to serve. God's vision for us will be a painting of the promise that moves us and motivates us in our ministry and keeps us true to fulfilling God's purpose. To see how all these factors coverge to bring God's vision into focus, let's look at some specific examples.

ZOE Ministry

God's vision can emerge at unexpected times from unexpected sources. So it was for Reverend Greg Jenks. One day in the fall of 2001, while Greg was serving as the founding pastor of a United Methodist church in North Carolina, a fifteen year old member of his congregation came to tell him about the cries of children from far away. This young lady opened Greg's ears to the cries of AIDS orphans in Africa, and as Greg states, "Somewhere deep in my spirit, an awakening began to occur."

For several years, Greg had sensed a change occurring in his own calling drawing him from service as a founding church pastor to service in the mission field. Greg's giftedness in apostleship, teaching, and encouragement had been powerfully employed, but a new passion had begun to stir. Greg says, "Over the next year and a half, a spark began flickering in my heart, ignited by the passion of Amanda Eckelkamp. By the end of July 2003, God had fanned that spark into a roaring fire within. That summer I came to two realizations. God had put a passion in my heart for the children of Africa. Children would die if I didn't go."

By January 2004, Greg and others took an exploratory trip to Zimbabwe, and within three months the Zimbabwe Orphan Endeavor (ZOE Ministry) was launched. To respond to the needs of millions of children who have been orphaned as a result of AIDS, Greg responded through his Burning Bush to begin a ministry that mobilizes many individual believers and churches to partner with the church in southern Africa. From this inter-section of needs and call, the vision of ZOE was birthed:

The physical and spiritual needs of orphaned African children being met by caring Christians from the United States.

Guided by this vision, ZOE employs four primary ministry strategies including:

- Feeding projects through which over 8,000 children regularly receive nutritional support
- School projects through which more that 1800 children receive school fees and clothing

- Summer camp projects which provide opportunities for worship, Bible study, music, and recreation

- Medical projects which provide voluntary medical care teams and needed pharmaceuticals.

Greg heard the cries of the orphans in Zimbabwe and responded through his God-given gifts, passion and joy. In the fullness of God's timing, ZOE was born. As a result of God's vision for ZOE and Greg, many others, too, are becoming instruments of God's healing for the broken and hurting children of southern Africa.

Car Care Ministry

Sometimes the cries of our neighbors come from thousands of miles away and sometimes from our own backyard. At first when a young married man learned that a single mom in his church did not have the resources to get her oil changed, he didn't think too much about it. After all, he could easily change the oil in her car and simply be helping out a friend. However, when the single mom responded that she knew several others in the same situation, the need suddenly loomed larger.

Sometimes our Vision is for neighbors far away... sometimes for the ones in our backyard.

Having the spiritual gifts of assisting, compassion, and encouragement, it came naturally for this young man to serve others through his mechanical skills. But God had also placed in his heart a real concern for single mothers and the daily challenges they face—seemingly simple challenges that can become insurmountable with limited money, time, and attention. Servicing their cars was one of those challenges. Thus a vision for ministry began to percolate among others in the men's group at Covenant Community United Methodist Church in Asheville, North Carolina, and within months Car Care was up and running.

From the intersection of the needs of single mothers (and others including older adults) and the gifts, passion and joy to respond to those needs, the vision for Car Care emerged:

Free basic car care provided for single mothers and older adults as an expression of Christ's love in servant ministry.

The Men's Ministry began to offer Car Care the first Saturday of every month to individuals throughout the community. Since 2001, the Car Care Ministry has provided basic auto work and service for no charge other than the cost of parts (for which scholarships are also available) to hundreds of single mothers and elderly neighbors. Additionally, the Women's Ministry at Covenant realized another great opportunity to minister by offering free child care, crafting classes, and transportation to shopping facilities while the people waited for their cars to be repaired. Not surprisingly, the church has embraced into the life of the congregation several new families who first came because of Car Care.

The Ministry of Plowpoint

Often times God's vision for us emerges in the midst of the fulfillment of another calling. As pastors, my husband and I had served several different churches in many different settings, and yet we noticed a commonality among them all. Regardless of the church's size or circumstances, each congregation struggled to some degree moving forward to claim God's promising future. We encountered recurring conflict, high turnover rates among staff, and worn out leadership. Additionally, Kelly and I, too, were struggling to hold everything together as we at times felt our marriage and ministries unraveling.

We heard the cries of our own churches yearning for something "more" but not knowing where or how to find it. Additionally, the cries of other congregations and leaders grew even louder as other pastors and congregations began to call us asking for help in regaining health and wholeness in their ministries.

Over time, we began to ask ourselves if God was specifically calling us to respond to the needs of churches and church leaders. God had given us the spiritual gifts of leadership, apostleship, teaching, prophecy, and discernment. God had prepared us in unique ways to go and assess the needs of the Body of Christ and to offer them healing through an equipping ministry of God's Word. Additionally, God had given us a deep passion for pastors and churches and a burning desire to see the Church become *fit for duty* to fulfill our calling as the Body of Christ. And amazingly, God gave us a sense of joy, even in the direst of circumstances. This joy was most aptly described by one of Plowpoint's team members one night after an intense session with a highly conflicted congregation. On her way home, Patty called to say in amazement, "This is crazy, but I love this work. I am so blessed these churches allow me to enter in and walk beside them through their darkest valleys of ministry."

The cries of churches and church leaders in need intersected with our gifts, passion, and joy to respond. And through the unique circumstances and experiences of a group of people (including backgrounds in the medical, teaching, and coaching fields) the vision for Plowpoint came into focus:

The Church prepared and repaired to be an effective instrument of healing for the broken and hurting world.

With increasing clarity of vision, the specific ministries of Plowpoint have emerged:
- Relational healing and the establishment of biblical boundaries for congregations in the midst of conflict

- Strategic visioning for congregations to claim God's right path and direction for their church
- Leadership and staff development to coalesce key leadership around God's vision and purpose for them
- Shepherd Care to equip, empower and nurture pastors to be healthy and effective shepherds among God's flock
- Sanctuary to create a sacred space for the healing and equipping of the church and church leaders in the context of worship and intercession.

Plowpoint's vision has become our guiding force, the picture of the Promise that motivates and moves us and keeps us true to what God desires.

In the Kingdom economy, no need is too small nor too great to be shaped into a God-sized vision. God fits the vision for us to suit our individual and corporate calling. Too often, though, our tendency is to trim down God's vision to make it fit our perceived abilities and resources. God's vision should be focused but never too contained. Barna reminds us that God's vision will stretch us "in every dimension: intellectually, spiritually, and emotionally." (*Turning Vision into Action*, 39)

Needs of
Our Neighbors

Our Unique
Ability to Respond

God's Vision or Another Good Idea?

When we begin to find the intersection of our neighbor's needs and our call to respond, the next valid question should be: **"Is this God's vision for us, or just another good idea?"** How do we distinguish between our good ideas for ministry and what may be a true vision and calling from God?

In God's economy, no need is too small or too great for a God-sized vision.

Barna offers a process for discerning God's vision using a series of seven checkpoints or steps (*Turning Vision into Action*, 40). As we apply these steps to a potential vision, we should regard each one as a hurdle or gateway through which we must pass before proceeding to the next. For example, we can not go to step two ("verified") if the idea is not "scriptural" (step one). For a potential vision to be deemed from God, it must pass through all seven steps. Listed below are the seven steps to which are added Scriptural references for additional guidance.

1. Scriptural

> *That very night the believers sent Paul and Silas to Berea. When they arrived there, they went to the synagogue. And the people of Berea were more open-minded than those in Thessalonica, and they listened eagerly to Paul's message. They searched the Scriptures day after day to check up on Paul and Silas, to see if they were really teaching the truth. As a result, many Jews believed, as did some of the prominent Greek women and many men.*
>
> **Acts 17:10-12 NLT**

God's will for us is always consistent with the Word, so if the vision is not consistent with Scripture, keep searching.

2. Verified

> *These things God has revealed to us through the Spirit; for the Spirit searches everything, even the depths of God. For what human being knows what is truly human except the human spirit that is within? So also no one comprehends what is truly God's except the Spirit of God. Now we have received not the spirit of the world, but the Spirit that is from God, so that we may understand the gifts bestowed on us by God. And we speak of these things in words not taught by human wisdom but taught by the Spirit, interpreting spiritual things to those who are spiritual.*
>
> *Those who are unspiritual do not receive the gifts of God's Spirit, for they are foolishness to them, and they are unable to understand them because they are spiritually discerned. Those who are spiritual discern all things, and they are themselves subject to no one else's scrutiny. "For who has known the mind of the Lord so as to instruct him?" But we have the mind of Christ.*

1 Corinthians 2:10-16 CEV

Meet with other trusted spiritual mentors or partners who are grounded in and led by God's Word and Spirit. Gain their counsel to see if this is God's vision for you or your ministry. If they have serious concerns, keep searching.

3. Emotion

> *Then Moses and Aaron fell facedown in front of the whole Israelite assembly gathered there. Joshua son of Nun and Caleb son of Jephunneh, who were among those who had explored the land, tore their clothes and said to the entire Israelite assembly, "The land we passed through and explored is exceedingly good. If the LORD is pleased with us, he will lead us into that land, a land flowing with milk and honey, and will give it to us. Only do not rebel against the LORD. And do not*

be afraid of the people of the land, because we will swallow them up. Their protection is gone, but the LORD is with us. Do not be afraid of them."

Numbers 14:5-9 NIV

True vision from God generates incredible enthusiasm and passion for the vision. Additionally, you should have a sense of anticipation of what God is going to do through this vision—regardless of the obstacles. If you are not truly excited and expectant about the vision, keep searching.

4. Fear

When the LORD saw that he had gone over to look, God called to him from within the bush, "Moses! Moses!" And Moses said, "Here I am." "Do not come any closer," God said. "Take off your sandals, for the place where you are standing is holy ground." Then he said, "I am the God of your father, the God of Abraham, the God of Isaac and the God of Jacob." At this, Moses hid his face, because he was afraid to look at God.

Exodus 3:4-6 NIV

When God reveals His vision to us, it is always "awesome." Awe is the perfect combination of wonder and fear that simultaneously draws us to the vision and makes us stand in fear of it. If you are not awed by the vision, keep searching.

5. Uniqueness

Then Esther told Hathach to go back and relay this message to Mordecai: "The whole world knows that anyone who appears before the king in his inner court without being invited is doomed to die unless the king holds out his gold scepter. And the king has not called for me to come to him in more than a month." So Hathuch gave Esther's message to Mordecai.

Mordecai sent back this reply to Esther: "Don't think for a moment that you will escape there in the palace when all the Jews are killed. If you keep quiet at a time like this, deliverance for the Jews will arise from some other place, but you and your relatives will die. What's more, who can say but that you have been elevated to the palace for just such a time as this?"

Esther 4:10-14 NLT

God's vision for us will be unique to our own particular giftedness, experience, resources, and circumstances. If this vision is not unique to you, keep searching.

6. Difficulty

But you must see that everything is done according to these plans. Be confident, and never be afraid of anything or get discouraged. The LORD my God will help you do everything needed to finish the temple, so it can be used for worshiping him. The priests and Levites have been assigned their duties, and all the skilled workers are prepared to do their work. The people and their leaders will do anything you tell them.

1 Chronicles 28:20-21 CEV

God's vision will always stretch us beyond what we could accomplish alone. God's vision will always require that we depend first and foremost on God and then on one another. If you think you can fulfill this vision on your own, keep searching.

7. Worthiness

From them on Jesus began to tell his disciples plainly that he had to go to Jerusalem, and he told them what would happen to him there. He would suffer at the hands of the leaders and the leading priests and the teachers of religious law. He would be killed, and he would be raised on the third day.

But Peter took him aside and corrected him. "Heaven forbid,

Lord," he said. "This will never happen to you!"

*Jesus turned to Peter and said, "Get away from me, Satan!
You are a dangerous trap to me. You are seeing things merely
from a human point of view, and not from God's"*

*Then Jesus said to the disciples, "If any of you wants to be my
follower, you must put aside your selfish ambition, shoulder
your cross, and follow me. If you try to keep your life for
yourself, you will lose it. But if you give up your life for me,
you will find true life."*

Matthew 16:21-25 NLT

God's vision for us is worthy of our fullest and deepest commitment. Would you sacrifice material and even intangible things for the sake of this vision? If not, keep searching.

Since this process is of human design (although biblically sound and God-inspired), it may be fallible. However, engaging in an intentional process of testing a vision for its Godly nature is both honorable and important if we are truly seeking to discern God's will. And even though a process such as this seems fairly straightforward, discerning God's vision for our lives and ministries rarely is. Instead, we must be committed to an ongoing process of *stepping in the stream* of God's will through the practice of the spiritual disciplines (Please see Chapter Four.) Then once the vision begins to unfold, we must commit to staying in the stream to test it and live it out.

Casting the Anchor–Firmly

Once we believe we have clarity regarding God's vision, we must cast that anchor firmly and speak it clearly so others can choose to follow.

*Then the LORD answered me and said:"Write the vision;
Make it plain on tablets, so that a runner may read it."*

Habakkuk 2:2 NRSV

When God's vision is revealed to us, we are also given the task of communicating that vision to others. After all, God's vision is always intended to reach beyond us and will require resources beyond our immediate reach. Therefore, we must be committed to communicating the vision clearly and firmly so others can coalesce, or NORM, around the vision and claim their part God is calling them to fulfill. In Chapter Ten, we will explore more fully this dynamic of casting the vision so others can give freely of themselves in the fulfillment of God's will.

But what happens if we cast the vision, but some people choose not to support the vision we believe is truly from God? When people are invited to NORM around the vision, it is simply that: an invitation. Most often not everyone will agree on the mission and vision and in fact, some may choose to part ways.

When we engage in an intentional process, rooted in the spiritual discipline of seeking God's will, and when we truly believe that God has given us clarity in that vision, then we must cast that anchor with great humility and boldness. Even then some people may disagree with the mission and vision and may choose to leave and not participate in the ministry. If so, we should release them with honor. Remember: **There is honor in staying, and there is honor in leaving as long as we stay or leave honorably.**

We must agree on the mission and God's vision for us—or choose to part ways.

On the other hand, there may be times when we are the ones who disagree with the mission or vision. We may find that we can not honor this vision, and therefore we can not with integrity submit to it. If so, our refusal to leave and any attempts to subvert the vision would be disruptive to God's work and be dishonorable.

To be effective in our ministry within the Body of Christ, we are called to have unity around the essentials that guide our life and ministry together. This would include the mission and vision to which God is calling us.

> *Now dear brothers and sisters, I appeal to you by the authority of the Lord Jesus Christ to stop arguing among yourselves. Let there be real harmony so there won't be divisions in the church. I plead with you to be of one mind, united in thought and purpose.*
> **1 Corinthians 1:10** NLT

Paul is reminding us that we must be united in our thought and purpose. We must agree on that which guides our life and ministry together. There may be many different ways through which we will accomplish God's vision, however these different means must always be harmonious or tuned

Jesus never undersold, softened, or miminized the vision. Neither should we.

to our common mission and vision that comes from God. If any of us refuses to tune to, or Norm around, God's mission and vision for us, we are at risk of causing disharmony and discord, and divisions may result that could greatly distract us from our Godly purpose.

Jesus humbly yet boldly cast the anchor for the vision of the Kingdom of Heaven given to him by God. This vision clearly defined Who Jesus was, Whose he was, and What God had sent him to accomplish. Jesus invited others to join him in this ministry. In fact, in many ways Jesus was dependent upon others

185

coalescing around this vision for the continuation of his ministry after his death. However, Jesus never undersold, minimized, or softened the vision for fear that some would not follow. To the contrary, Jesus articulated the vision with increasing clarity regarding the cost and sacrifice required to fulfill it.

> *Jesus felt genuine love for this man as he looked at him. "You lack only one thing," he told him. "Go and sell all you have and give the money to the poor, and you will have treasure in heaven. Then come and follow me." At this, the man's face fell, and he went away sadly because he had many possessions.*
>
> *Jesus looked around and said to his disciples, "How hard it is for rich people to get into the Kingdom of God!" This amazed them. But Jesus said again, "Dear children, it is very hard to get into the Kingdom of God. It is easier for a camel to go through the eye of a needle than for a rich person to enter the Kingdom of God!"*
>
> **Mark 10:21-25** NLT

Despite the material possessions the rich young ruler could offer to their ministry, Jesus did not minimize the cost to follow the vision or alter the vision to make it more appealing. Like Jesus, we too must be committed to casting the anchor humbly, yet boldly. We must trust that if the vision is God-given, then God will raise up the people and the resources to carry forth the vision in obedience. Some may deny the vision. Some may even betray it. But by God's grace, some will be obedient to it so that God's purpose will be fulfilled no matter what the cost.

Questions for Discussion

1. As we compare the needs of our neighbors (next door and/or far away) with our unique calling to respond, where do we find these intersecting?

2. What excites or motivates us about how God may use us at this "intersection" to be instruments of God's grace?

3. How might we articulate or "write the vision plainly" so others can understand it and know what our minsitry is about (and is not about)?

4. How will we move boldly (and yet humbly) forward in obedience to the vision when others refuse to follow?

The Right Next Step for Chapter Nine

In Chapter Nine, you will focus on ways to put your vision into action through specific ministry programs or strategies. Begin praying and thinking this week about ways in which this vision can become real. Apply the seven steps or checkpoints to each of the possible strategies. Come prepared to share these with others the next time you gather.

Scripture and Prayers
Day 1
Exodus 3:8
So I have come down to rescue them from the hand of the Egyptians and to bring them out of that land into a good and spacious land, a land flowing with milk and honey...
Isaiah 65:17, 24-25
"Behold I will create a new heaven and a new earth. The former things will not be remembered, nor will they come to mind... Before they call, I will answer, while they are still speaking, I will hear. The wolf and the lamb will feed together, and the lion will eat straw like an ox..." says the Lord.

Focus Notes

Lord, you have given us a promise and a hope of what shall be. Help us be faithful to the journey along the way and to remember that we are a part of your design and plan to bring about change and restoration in the midst of it. Let us not lose sight of the big picture, and let us not lose sight of our piece of it. Help us claim that part to which we are called to show to the world.

Day 2
Genesis 12:1-3
The Lord said to Abram, "Leave your country, your people, and your father's household, and go up to the land I will show you. I will make you into a great nation and bless you; I will make your name great, and you will be a blessing...all the peoples on earth will blessed through you."

Genesis 15:5-6
He took him outside and said, "Look up at the heavens and count the stars---if you can count them." Then he said to him, "So shall your offspring be." Abraham believed the Lord and he credited it to him as righteousness.

Focus Notes

God, you have given us a mission and a purpose. Remind us daily that it is your vision and your direction that lead us and not our own desires. Help us stay true to the path to which you have called us and not be distracted by the many other "good" paths along the way. Let us not use our time, energy, and resources on the good path but the God path.

Day 3
Genesis 8:10
Then the Lord said, "I will surely return to you about this same time next year, and Sarah your wife will have a son..."

Lord, help us stay true to the vision even when it seems a long time in coming. Help us not abandon or seek short cuts along the path. Help us remember that you are true and that your promises are true. Help us not grow weary in waiting, but eagerly prepare for the birth of the vision as it grows and matures. Let us not try to give birth prematurely but wait for the appointed time.

Focus Notes

Day 4
Genesis 41:39-40, 53-54, 57
Then Pharaoh said to Joseph, "Since God has made all this known to you, there is no one as discerning and wise as you. You shall be in charge of my palace and all my people are to submit to your orders...The seven years of abundance in Egypt came to an end and the seven years of famine began, just as Joseph had said. There was famine in all other lands, but in the land of Egypt there was food. And all the others countries came to Egypt to buy grain from Joseph, because the famine was severe in all the world.

God, help us remember that where you place us, you will use us. You will use our gifts as a people to bless others and to save others. Help us not become blind to those in our midst or blind to the setting in which you place us. Help us continually focus on who we are, where we are, and what we have been given. You will use all of these to fulfill your purpose for us as a church and for the world around us.

Day 5
Luke 9:22
And he said, "The Son of man must suffer many things and be rejected by the elders, chief priests and the teachers of the law, and he must be killed and on the third day be raised to life."

Luke 24: 17-21
Jesus asked them, "What were you talking about as you walked along?" The two of them stood there looking sad and gloomy. Then the one named Cleopas asked Jesus, "Are you the only person from Jerusalem who didn't know what was happening there these last few days?" "What do you mean?" Jesus asked. They answered: "Those things that happened to Jesus from Nazareth. By what he did and said he showed that he was a powerful prophet, who pleased God and all the people. Then the chief priests and our leaders had him arrested and sentenced to die on a cross. We had hoped that he would be the one to set Israel free! But it has already been three days since all this

> **Focus Notes**

happened." CEV

God, your vision and our understanding of it may not always coincide. It may seem too ominous for us or stretch our understanding beyond what we are accustomed. Keep us hopeful and determined even when it seems beyond us and our understanding or abilities. Never let us lose hope even when others try to quench that hope. You are faithful and the Author and Finisher of our faith.

Focus Notes

Day 6

Numbers 13:30-32

Caleb calmed down the crowd and said, "Let's go and take the land. I know we can do it!" But the other men replied, "Those people are much too strong for us." Then they started spreading rumors and saying, "We won't be able to grow anything in that soil. And the people are like giants." CEV

Lord, help us 0communicate the vision clearly and boldly. Let us not be intimidated by the size of it nor the nay-sayers among us. Help us to write it plain and BOLDLY and to cast a firm anchor that will not be moved by others nor waves and words of doubt.

Day 7
John 6:54-56, 60, 66-67
"Whoever eats my flesh and drinks my blood has eternal life, and I will raise him up on the last day. For my flesh is real food and my blood is real drink…On hearing this, many of his disciples said, "This is a hard teaching. Who can accept it?"…From this time, many of his disciples turned back and no longer followed him. "You do not want to leave too?" Jesus asked the twelve.

Jesus, help us remember that your call and your vision is unique to us all, even as a group. Sometimes it is a hard vision and call to follow. Help us stay unified around that to which you have called us, even when we can't all agree. Let us not be a stumbling block in the path of your vision for a particular group. Give us the grace and the mercy to part ways if it is not what we feel called to do, and give us the grace and mercy to release those who feel the need to go. Give us spirits of humility to honor one another where we are led even if it is on a totally different path.

Trust in the Lord
with all your heart;
do not depend
on your own
understanding.
Seek his will
in all you do,
And he will direct
your paths.
Proverbs 3:5-6

| Nine |

| Strategizing the Vision |

Once we firmly cast the anchor of our mission and vision thus clarifing WHAT God has called us to do, we can finally PERFORM the ministries God has sent us to accomplish. When our PERFORMING is consistent with our God-given mission and vision, our ministries will involve doing incredible God-things. Furthermore, when we are obedient to our vision, we may need to let go of doing some good things that are inconsistent with the anchor we have cast.

What we do in our ministries should always be consistent with our mission and our vision. In other words, our mission and vision should become the common pitch to which all our ministry strategies are tuned. If a particular program or strategy would be helpful in fulfilling our mission and vision, then it is worthy to consider, but if it is inconsistent with our mission and vision, then our resources (time, money, attention, personnel) should be used in other ways. To accomplish God's will, God will provide us everything we need. However, we should not expect God to provide for our efforts beyond what God has called us to do.

Planning for the Vision

At the beginning of our study, we discussed how planning is both honorable and crucial as long as our planning follows the discernment of God's will. The appropriate time and place for planning is once we have clarity in God's vision. Discernment of God's mission and vision for us determines WHAT we are to do to bring about God's Kingdom. Planning for our ministries determines How we will accomplish the mission and vision God has called us to fulfill.

To PERFORM in our ministries, we must consider several different aspects of planning. First, we must develop strategies or ministry approaches that will put the vision into action. Any given ministry may have several different ministry strategies that will answer the question: "How will we fulfill this vision?"

Looking again at a ministry example from Chapter Eight, let's consider the specific strategies employed by the ZOE Ministry to carry out their vision:

- Feeding projects to provide nutritional support.
- School projects to provide school fees and clothing.
- Summer camp projects to provide opportunities for worship, Bible study, music and recreation.
- Medical projects to provide volunteer medical teams and pharmaceuticals.

Every program or event we offer becomes a specific means by which our vision is put into action.

These four strategies are specific approaches to fulfill ZOE Ministry's vision:

The physical and spiritual needs of orphaned African children being met by caring Christians from the United States.

Another way to think about strategies would be the development of specific programs or events. When our strategies flow from our mission and vision, every program or event we offer becomes a specific means by which our vision is put into action. Remember: if it's not consistent with our mission and vision, then we don't need to do it—because we're not called to do it! To illustrate this dynamic more fully, let's explore the possibilities of ministry for a fictitious (but very realistic) church: Bible Fellowship Church.

Strategizing the Vision for Bible Fellowship

Bible Fellowship is a fifty year old church located in Anywhere, USA, a small but growing suburban town. Anywhere, for many years, was primarily a mill town whose citizens worked and lived within a few miles of the town limits. However, during the past two decades, many of the mills have closed, and the local industry has changed. Likewise, the citizens and neighborhoods of Anywhere have also changed. Many of the residents rush from one activity to the other and seem to have little time to connect with family, friends, much less church.

Bible Fellowship Church began as a neighborhood church that was formerly well connected with their neighbors and community. But increasingly over the past several years, many of the adult children have moved away from the neighborhood and the church. As a result, Bible Fellowship is now often described as an aging and dwindling congregation. However, a few new young families have recently joined, and some others have returned "back home."

Bible Fellowship also has many active adults, many who are retired and have much to offer the church and community. Additionally, one of the strongest aspects of Bible Fellowship throughout the years has been their passionate commitment for teaching God's Word, and yet Sunday School attendance has dropped drastically in recent years. Like many churches, Bible Fellowship is concerned about remaining both viable and vibrant in their commitment to the Great Commission of making disciples for Jesus Christ. But recently, they are unclear how to make this happen.

During the past several months, the leadership of Bible Fellowship engaged in an intentional process to discern God's vision and direction for them as a congregation. Each of the leaders committed to set aside time every day for Bible study and prayer seeking clarity in God's will and plan for them. Additionally, they came together once a week to dwell with one another and to share how God is speaking to each of them individually. They reviewed together their history as a church, and each one shared how and when they became a part of the unfolding story of God working in their midst. And they entered into a relational covenant with one another that provides healthy boundaries to protect their relationships and life in ministry together.

The leadership of Bible Fellowship also conducted a demographic study of the community and met with people in the church and community to discover the needs of their neighbors.

To truly hear our calling, we must listen to God and the people and not just the statistics.

Repeatedly, the leadership heard that people feel disconnected from one another and even the church, and the church feels disconnected from the community. Many families in the community reported having few, if any, opportunities to be with other families or friends. Instead, they feel their lives are filled with demands of work, school, and simply making ends meet. Demographically, the leadership learned that Anywhere has a growing number of single parent households, and in most two parent households, both parents work outside the home. The leadership was also disappointed (but not surprised) to learn that few people have a solid, if any, working knowledge of Scripture, and very few people are actively involved in regular Bible study.

In addition to discovering the needs of their neighbors, the group also found they have been uniquely prepared to respond.

Through spiritual gift inventories of the congregation, the leadership learned that three primary gifts repeatedly emerged among the members: hospitality, teaching, and encouragement. As they talked about what burdened and excited them the most, the leadership also claimed their passion for offering and teaching Bible studies, opening their church and homes to people in ways that make others feel welcome and comfortable, and wanting people to know that they can make a difference in the world. The leadership was also in agreement that Bible Fellowship Church is in a great place to reach many families since they are located close to commuter routes between work and school.

Pay attention to key concepts or common threads that emerge as we find the intersection.

From the intersection of their neighbors' needs and their unique abilities and setting to respond, Bible Fellowship has discerned God's vision for their church to be the following:

"A church connecting people to the Word, one another, and the needs of the world."

When the leadership was ready to put the vision into action, they began by asking the key questions: "How will we connect people to the Word? To one another? To the needs of the world?"

From these questions, the leadership began to brainstorm several program options that would fulfill the vision, and the following strategies emerged:

- Small group gatherings offering weekly Bible study in homes throughout the community and providing simple meals (and childcare, if needed) in conjunction with the study.

- Welcoming Worshipers extending hospitality to all worshipers on Sunday mornings. Intentional emphasis would be on personally connecting with visitors and irregular attenders by being present to them throughout worship and following up with them during the week.
- Afterschool and holiday care for students in the community including transportation from school to church. A meal and opportunity for Bible study for families would also be offered once a week at the church following pickup of the students.
- Mission support (financial and prayer) for a missionary couple (formerly from Anywhere) who serve as international Bible translators.

In addition to suggesting these new ministry strategies, the leadership also reviewed existing programs. As a result, they discovered that some of the current programs at the church needed to be discontinued due to inconsistency with the vision and lack of leadership, participation and enthusiasm.

Surveying the Situation

Once we have identified key strategies and programs which will put our vision into action, we should prepare for the tasks. This is where planning can be critically important. Our new enthusiasm to charge boldly ahead can be thwarted by unseen pitfalls. The writer of Proverbs warns us:

> *A prudent person foresees the danger ahead and takes precautions; the simpleton goes blindly on and suffers the consequences.* **Proverbs 22:3 NLT**

Undoubtedly, we want to fuel our zeal for performing in our ministries, but the way of the wise requires us to survey the situation to see what lies ahead. One reliable process for analyzing a particular strategy is called the **SWOT** analysis. Using SWOT, we identify our STRENGTHS, WEAKNESSES, OPPORTUNITIES, and THREATS in implementing each strategy. For any strategy or program being considered, we should ask:

- What STRENGTHS do we have that would help us implement this strategy?
- What WEAKNESSES do we have that could make implementation of this strategy difficult?
- What OPPORTUNITIES would this strategy potentially open up or provide?
- What THREATS are potentially present that could thwart this ministry effort?

All four questions should be openly and honestly addressed by the leaders involved in the ministry, and concerns regarding resistance should never prevent us from asking these critical questions. After all, it is much better to be aware of and prepared for potential obstacles before they occur. In this way, the SWOT analysis can provide a more detailed road map that identifies the twists, turns, and roadblocks that could be ahead.

Surveying the Exodus Journey
In the Exodus story, God gave Moses the clear vision for a preferable future for the Israelites:

> "The people of God freed from bondage
> living in a land of promise."

One primary strategy that would answer the How this vision would become reality was Moses leading the people out of Egypt. But before the Exodus could begin, God and Moses had an intense dialogue that identified the STRENGTHS, WEAKNESSES, OPPORTUNITIES, and THREATS Moses and the Israelites would encounter. The dialogue is found in Exodus 3:16-4:17.

[16]"Now go and call together all the leaders of Israel. Tell them, 'The LORD, the God of your ancestors—the God of Abraham, Isaac, and Jacob—appeared to me in a burning bush. He said, "You can be sure that I am watching over you and have seen what is happening to you in Egypt. [17] I promise to rescue you from the oppression of the Egyptians. I will lead you to the land now occupied by the Canaanites, Hittites, Amorites, Perizzites, Hivites, and Jebusites—a land flowing with milk and honey."'

[18]"The leaders of the people of Israel will accept your message. Then all of you must go straight to the king of Egypt and tell him, 'The LORD, the God of the Hebrews, has met with us. Let us go on a three-day journey into the wilderness to offer sacrifices to the LORD our God.' [19]"But I know that the king of Egypt will not let you go except under heavy pressure. [20] So I will reach out and strike at the heart of Egypt with all kinds of miracles. Then at last he will let you go. [21] And I will see to it that the Egyptians treat you well. They will load you down with gifts so you will not leave empty-handed. [22] The Israelite women will ask for silver and gold jewelry and fine clothing from their Egyptian neighbors and their neighbors' guests. With this clothing, you will dress your sons and daughters. In this way, you will plunder the Egyptians!"

[1]But Moses protested again, "Look, they won't believe me! They won't do what I tell them. They'll just say, 'The LORD never appeared to you.'" [2] Then the LORD asked him, "What do you have there in your hand?" "A shepherd's staff," Moses replied. [3]"Throw it down on the ground," the LORD told him. So Moses threw it down, and it became a snake! Moses was terrified, so he turned and ran away. [4] Then the LORD told him, "Take hold of its tail." So Moses reached out and grabbed it, and it became a shepherd's staff again. [5]"Perform this sign, and they will believe you," the LORD told him. "Then they will realize that the LORD, the God of their ancestors—the God of Abraham, the God of Isaac, and the God of Jacob—really has appeared to you." [6] Then the LORD said to Moses,

"Put your hand inside your robe." Moses did so, and when he took it out again, his hand was white as snow with leprosy. [7]"Now put your hand back into your robe again," the Lord said. Moses did, and when he took it out this time, it was as healthy as the rest of his body. [8]"If they do not believe the first miraculous sign, they will believe the second," the Lord said. [9]"And if they do not believe you even after these two signs, then take some water from the Nile River and pour it out on the dry ground. When you do, it will turn into blood." [10]But Moses pleaded with the Lord, "O Lord, I'm just not a good speaker. I never have been, and I'm not now, even after you have spoken to me. I'm clumsy with words." [11]"Who makes mouths?" the Lord asked him. "Who makes people so they can speak or not speak, hear or not hear, see or not see? Is it not I, the Lord? [12]Now go, and do as I have told you. I will help you speak well, and I will tell you what to say." [13]But Moses again pleaded, "Lord, please! Send someone else." [14]Then the Lord became angry with Moses. "All right," he said. "What about your brother, Aaron the Levite? He is a good speaker. And look! He is on his way to meet you now. And when he sees you, he will be very glad. [15]You will talk to him, giving him the words to say. I will help both of you to speak clearly, and I will tell you what to do. [16]Aaron will be your spokesman to the people, and you will be as God to him, telling him what to say. [17]And be sure to take your shepherd's staff along so you can perform the miraculous signs I have shown you."

Exodus 3:16-4:17 NLT

As with many of us, Moses was quick to point out first the weaknesses and threats they would face, including his own inability to speak (4:10) and his fear that no one would believe him or respond (4:1). Of course, God was also realistic and honest in acknowledging the pressures and resistance Moses would encounter. However, the weaknesses and threats of Moses were followed with the reminder that in the face of their weaknesses God would make them strong. Moses was reminded that God would watch over them (3:16), rescue them (3:17) as well as provide for them (3:21-22). To every concern Moses raised in carrying out this strategy, God promised to turn the weaknesses into strengths (4:11-12) and the threats to opportunities (4:1-9).

So often when we perceive weaknesses or threats in implementing our ministries, we avoid the ministry altogether. However, Paul reminds us that the weaknesses and threats we face often become opportunities for Christ's power to be made strong in and through us.

> *But to keep me from getting puffed up, I was given a thorn in my flesh, a messenger from Satan to torment me and keep me from getting proud. Three different times I begged the Lord to take it away. Each time he said, "My gracious favor is all you need. My power works best in your weakness." So now I am glad to boast about my weakness, so that the power of Christ may work through me.*
>
> **1 Corinthians 12:7-9** NLT

God's grace in and for our ministries is sufficient to convert our weaknesses to strengths and our threats to opportunities. However, we must first intentionally assess and acknowledge what those obstacles could be so we can offer those areas to the Lord for removal and redemption. Of course, our own wise and faithful action may also be expected and required to make the conversions as well. God may require us to involve other servants who strengths will cover our weaknesses as Aaron did for Moses (4:14-16).

God converts our weaknesses to strengths and our threats to opportunities.

Likewise, God often requires us to use what God has given us with the faith that God can and will act through it. So it was with the shepherd's staff. It was critically important for Moses to be aware of the potential threats they would face. To respond to the threats (disbelief, resistance, even walls of water), God gave Moses a shepherd's staff. But for the staff to do any good Moses would have to use it with faith!

And be sure to take your shepherd's staff along so you can perform the miraculous signs I have shown you.

Exodus 4:17 NLT

Through the staff God had given him and the faith required to use it, Moses turned many threats into opportunities for demonstrating God's great power and might. And it was this same power and might that would ultimately ensure their release from bondage and arrival in the Promised Land.

But what happens if our SWOT analysis of a strategy uncovers more weaknesses than strengths and more threats than opportunities? We wait, and we pray before acting. Any strategy, like the vision, may be the right one in the fullness of God's timing. However we must be wise and faithful stewards of the vision by continuing to look for what God has already given us and to wait for what God has yet to provide. Throughout the Exodus story, when faced with obstacles and threats, Moses cried out to God for help making the needs clearly known. And in the fullness of God's timing, God worked through and among those chosen people to overcome obstacles, foreseen and unseen.

If a vision is from God we will need the help of God and others to fulfill it.

Sharing the Blessings (and Burdens)

God's vision for our ministries will always require the faithful efforts and commitment of several, if not many, individuals. If a vision is of God, it will require the partnership of many. As we heard in the story of King David and the instructions for building the Lord's Temple (1 Chronicles 28:20-21), the task would require the skills and efforts of many groups of people who would follow the directions of the leaders in obedience to God.

Fulfilling God's will through our ministries is truly a blessing, but when attempted alone, it can be an unmanageable burden. God surrounded Moses with Aaron and Miriam who would work with him to lead the Exodus. But as the scope of the ministry and tasks expanded, the need for a larger ministry team also grew.

The next day Moses took his seat to serve as judge for the people, and they stood around him from morning till evening. When his father-in-law saw all that Moses was doing for the people, he said, "What is this you are doing for the people? Why do you alone sit as judge, while all these people stand around you from morning till evening?"

Moses answered him, "Because the people come to me to seek God's will. Whenever they have a dispute, it is brought to me, and I decide between the parties and inform them of God's decrees and laws."

Moses' father-in-law replied, "What you are doing is not good. You and these people who come to you will only wear yourselves out. The work is too heavy for you; you cannot handle it alone. Listen now to me and I will give you some advice, and may God be with you. You must be the people's representative before God and bring their disputes to him. Teach them the decrees and laws, and show them the way to live and the duties they are to perform. But select capable men from all the people—men who fear God, trustworthy men who hate dishonest gain—and appoint them as officials over thousands, hundreds, fifties and tens. Have them serve as judges for the people at all times, but have them bring every difficult case to you; the simple cases they can decide themselves. That will make your load lighter, because they will share it with you. If you do this and God so commands, you will be able to stand the strain, and all these people will go home satisfied."

Exodus 18:13-23 NIV

Many of us can probably relate to Moses and his burgeoning work among the people. Moses, like many of us, was trying to do it all alone. He was so busy trying to respond to the needs, he didn't realize there was any other option! But his father-in-law, Jethro, was observing Moses and could foresee the negative impact on both the people and Moses if the load was not distributed. Jethro could see that unless others were involved in this ministry, Moses would wear out and the people would become increasingly disgruntled. So in response to this need, Jethro suggested the development of a ministry team that would both optimize the abilities of many people and provide long term viability for the ministry.

Any ministry strategy or program deserves the attention and work of a ministry team to ensure its stability and viability. Following Jethro's wise guidance, we too should establish ministry teams that utilize individuals according to their gifts and abilities. Each team should have a leader that provides both spiritual and logistical direction, and each team member should be capable, honest, and desiring to serve God in the accomplishment of the tasks.

Every valid ministry requires a ministry team. Jesus didn't do it alone—why should we?

But how do we determine who and how many we need on the team? Once the specific programs or strategies are identified, we likewise determine the specific tasks and functions involved in each program. Functions may then be grouped into ministry position descriptions which describe the specific functions and abilities needed to perform that aspect of the ministry (such as teacher, group facilitator, cook, or musician). Once we have identified all the positions needed, we begin to pray for God to raise up those persons with the BURNING BUSH (the gifts, passion and joy for that function) to fulfill this particular need. As those people come together, they form the ministry team required for this strategy.

But what if those people do not come forward, and the ministry team does not come together? We continue to pray, and we wait as we continually and consistently make the need known to the church and to God. Again, if any ministry is essential in fulfilling God's will for us, then God will answer our requests and in due time, the people will respond. On the other hand, if we move ahead without waiting for the right people to fulfill the right functions based on their BURNING BUSH, we, like Moses, will be at risk of burning out. Additionally, discontent can result within us, the ministry, and the church. Having to wait should not necessarily be translated as God's "No" to a ministry strategy. However, it may indicate, "Not now."

Stepping in, and remaining in, the stream of God's will requires a constant balance of moving boldly and waiting patiently. Knowing when it is time to move or to wait requires trust—trusting God's presence, protection, and provision in our ministries so we don't fall behind nor get ahead of God.

Questions for Discussion

1. What are specific ways we can put our vision into action? Brainstorm various ministry strategies or program ideas to put feet, hands and heart to the vision. Prioritize the possible strategies based on enthusiasm, impact, and importance.

2. What are potential STRENGTHS, WEAKNESSES, OPPORTUNITIES, and THREATS associated with each strategy? Make a chart for each.

3. What kind of ministry team would we need for each strategy or program? List the important Spiritual Gifts, Passion and Joy in Ministry that would be needed for members of the team.

The Right Next Step for Chapter Ten

Once you have identified specific ministry strategies, you have a clearer understanding of what will be needed to accomplish the ministry tasks. For each of the top prioritized strategies, begin making a list of resources which may be needed to accomplish this strategy including personnel (paid and/or unpaid), time, space, money, and materials.

Continue to pray daily for God to reveal the fullness of God's vision for you so there will be full provision for the ministry.

Scripture & Prayers

Day 1
Numbers 13:17-20
Before Moses sent them into Canaan, he said: "After you go through the Southern Desert of Canaan, continue north into the hill country and find out what those regions are like. Be sure to remember how many people live there, how strong they are, and if they live in open towns or walled cities. See if the land is good for growing crops and find out what kinds of trees grow there. It's time for grapes to ripen, so try to bring back some of the fruit that grows there." CEV

Focus Notes

Lord, give us wisdom and knowledge of where we are going and where you want to take us. Give us the foresight to survey what lies ahead. Open our eyes to a full picture of the situation before us. Help us identify the potential strengths and weaknesses, the opportunities and the threats. When we do this with boldness and faith, you prepare the way before us, and we can prepare for any obstacles or difficult places along the way. Your Holy Spirit moves before us like a banner to prepare the way. Thank you for your Spirit.

Day 2
Judges 6:14-15
Then the LORD himself said, "Gideon, you will be strong, because I am giving you the power to rescue Israel from the Midianites." Gideon replied, "But how can I rescue Israel? My clan is the weakest one in Manasseh, and everyone else in my family is more important than I am." CEV

Jeremiah 1:4-7
Now the word of the Lord came to me saying, "Before I formed you in the womb I knew you, and before you were born I consecrated you; I appointed you a prophet to the nations." Then I said, "Ah, Lord God! Truly I do not know how to speak, for I am only a boy." But the Lord said to me, "Do not say, 'I am only a boy;' for you shall go to all to whom I send you, and you shall speak whatever I command you." NRSV

Focus Notes

Sovereign Lord, let us not be intimidated or paralyzed by our weakness. Remind us that if you send us, you will equip us for every good work. Help us remember that our weakness is only an opportunity for you to work through us so that you may be glorified and our faith may grow.

Day 3

Exodus 17:1-2, 5-6

They camped at Rephidim, but there was no water for the people to drink. So they quarreled with Moses and said, "Give us water to drink."...The Lord answered Moses, "Walk on ahead of the people. Take some of the elders of Israel and take in your hand the staff which you struck the Nile and go. I will stand there before you by the rock at Horeb. Strike the rock and water will come out for the people to drink." NIV

Focus Notes

Mighty God, help us to see the perceived threats among us as opportunities for you to work. Give us the faith to believe your Word and Promises, and empower us to act boldly and to use that which you have given us. You have given us everything we need to carry out your call. No matter how simple and rudimentary it is, in your hands working through us, all things are possible. Seas will part and water will gush forth in the wilderness. Keep our eyes open to your wondrous works. Keep us from resorting to complaints. You are a wonderful God!

Day 4
Deuteronomy 1:9-13
At that time I said to you, "I am unable by myself to bear you. The Lord your God has multiplied you, so that today you are as numerous as the stars of heaven. May the Lord, the God of your ancestors, increase you a thousand times more and bless you, as he has promised you! But how can I bear the heavy burden of your disputes all by myself? Choose for each of your tribes individuals who are wise, discerning, and reputable to be your leaders." NRSV

Focus Notes

Lord, give us the ability to wisely delegate responsibilities and tasks. You did not intend or expect us to do ministry alone. Show us how to equip and empower others for ministry so that it may grow and flourish. You have blessed us all with many talents and abilities. Teach us how to use them in concert with one another and in concert with your plan and vision for us. Then we will accomplish even greater works for you. Strengthen our understanding of spiritual gifts and their use in the Body of Christ. Open our eyes to your work.

Day 5
Judges 7:4
But the Lord said to Gideon, "There are still too many men.
Take them down to the water, and I will sift them for you there.
If I say 'This one shall go with you,' he shall go; but if I say 'This
one shall not go with you,' he shall not go." NIV

Lord, you know who is called to minister and who is not. You see the heart and passion that we cannot always see. Help us trust you to bring those forth that you have called and not those that we would call. Give us the spiritual eyes to see as you see and not with just flesh and human nature.

Focus Notes

Day 6
Acts 13:1-3
In the church in Antioch, there
were prophets and teachers:
Barnabas, Simon called Niger,
Lucius of Cyrene, Manaen,
and Saul. While they were
worshipping the Lord and
fasting the Holy Spirit said, "Set apart for me Barnabas and
Saul for the work to which I have called them." So after they
had fasted and prayed, they placed their hands on them and sent
them off. NIV

214

God, give us the discipline to fast and pray for those you desire to use. Let us not take it lightly, but let it be a burden to us as it was to you. Let us be active in coming to you and to the Body with our needs in ministry. The servants are there, Lord, prepare their hearts for the work of your Kingdom. Help their spirits know your voice when you call and help us know how to speak the call.

Day 7
Acts 1:4

While he was still with them, he said: "Don't leave Jerusalem yet. Wait here for the Father to give you the Holy Spirit, just as I told you he has promised to do." CEV

Focus Notes

Jesus, help us wait. We are a people of immediacy and impatience. Teach us to know the leading of your Spirit so that we move only by your bidding. Do not let us move from under the cloud and shadow of your protection and provision. Your timing is perfect. Help us

Trust in the Lord
with all your heart;
do not depend
on your own
understanding.
Seek his will
in all you do,
And he will direct
your paths.
Proverbs 3:5-6

Ten

Trusting God's Provision

*I*t just seems too simple and too good to be true: To fulfill God's will everything we need will be provided. In a world that insists on a paradigm of scarcity, God's Word persists with a paradigm of abundance.

> *And God is able to provide you with every blessing in abundance, so that by always having enough of everything, you may share abundantly in every good work.*
>
> **2 Corinthians 9:8 NRSV**

If our ministry is consistent with God's mission and vision for us, we will have sufficient resources to accomplish it. So, if this is true, why does it seem there is never enough time, money, people, or space to do what we need to do? The key is in understanding what provision really is and in trusting and waiting on God for that provision.

Pro-Vision

Jesus teaches us that if we set our sights on God's Kingdom, then God will provide for our needs:

> *Your heavenly Father already knows all your needs, and he will give you all you need from day to day if you live for him and make the Kingdom of God your primary concern.*
>
> **Matthew 6:32-33 NLT**

If our lives and our ministries exist to bring about the Kingdom of God, then God will give us what we need to make it so. However, Jesus also reminds us that to receive what we need, we must first ask.

Ask, and it will be given you; search, and you will find; knock, and the door will be opened for you. For everyone who asks receives, and everyone who searches finds, and for everyone who knocks, the door will be opened.

Matthew 7:7-8 NRSV

Therefore, God's provision is in part dependent on our asking, but we also need to know how to ask.

From the beginning of Plowpoint, we prayed for God's provision for our ministry pressing into God for our needs. But one day as I was praying, God impressed on me, "Beth, break it down. What does it mean to ask for My provision?" Then it occurred to me what provision really is:

**Pro+Vision = that which is in favor of
or in support of the Vision.**

God's Word persists with a paradigm of abundance.

I realized that before we could ask God for specific needs, we first needed clarity in God's vision for our ministry. If we limited God's vision for us, then we could limit God's provision. So we began to pray asking God for clarity in the fullness of God's vision to ensure that we would receive the fullness of God's provision.

Scripture repeatedly tells us that we have not because we ask not and that if we ask in accordance with God's will, our requests will be granted.

Stay joined to me and let my teachings become part of you. Then you can pray for whatever you want, and your prayer will be answered.

John 15:7 CEV

Furthermore, Scripture reminds us that God also provides for our needs through the offerings of other people. In Exodus, we hear the story of God's vision for building the Tabernacle as revealed to Moses:

> *Then have them make a sanctuary for me, and I will dwell among them. Make this tabernacle and all its furnishings exactly like the pattern I will show you.*
>
> **Exodus 25:8-9 NIV**

As Moses sought to fulfill God's vision for the Tabernacle, he received incredible clarity from God regarding what would be needed in materials and skills to do so. And once Moses understood the scope of the vision and the specifics of the needs, Moses clearly communicated both of these to the people.

When God gives us clarity in the vision for our ministries, we must communicate to others what God desires. We must paint a picture of the promise God has set before us so others can choose to take part. And once people's hearts and imaginations are stirred, they too will understand the part they are to play in fulfilling the vision.

We must communicate clearly what is needed to fulfill the vision.

In Exodus 35, Moses described thoroughly to the people God's vision and instructions for constructing the Tabernacle. Moses invited and encouraged the people to participate in the vision by calling forth their skills and material possessions. Then in response to Moses casting the vision and asking them to take part, the people responded.

> *Then the whole Israelite community withdrew from Moses' presence, and everyone who was willing and whose heart moved him came and brought an offering to the LORD for the*

work on the Tent of Meeting, for all its service, and for the sacred garments....

Every skilled woman spun with her hands and brought what she had spun—blue, purple or scarlet yarn or fine linen. And all the women who were willing and had the skill spun the goat hair....

Then Moses said to the Israelites, "See, the LORD has chosen Bezalel son of Uri, the son of Hur, of the tribe of Judah, and he has filled him with the Spirit of God, with skill, ability and knowledge in all kinds of crafts to make artistic designs for work in gold, silver and bronze, to cut and set stones, to work in wood and to engage in all kinds of artistic crafts- manship. And he has given both him and Oholiab son of Ahisamach, of the tribe of Dan, the ability to teach others. He has filled them with skill to do all kinds of work as craftsmen, designers, embroiderers in blue, purple and scarlet yarn and fine linen, and weavers—all of them master craftsmen and designers.

Exodus 35:20-21, 25-26, & 30-35 NIV

Not everyone who heard the vision and request to help respond- ed by doing so. However, those who did catch the vision and were convicted by the Holy Spirit gave of themselves readily and freely in both their material possessions and their time and skills.

> *The most common mistake is failure to ask—and to ask specifically for what is needed.*

Common wisdom and practice tells us that the most common mistake made in fundraising efforts is the failure to ask and to ask specifically for what is needed. Moses knew precisely what was needed, so he told the Israelites and asked them to participate. But not everyone responded. However, the response was sufficient. In fact, it was more than was needed.

Then Moses gave an order and they sent this word through-
out the camp: "No man or woman is to make anything else
as an offering for the sanctuary." And so the people were
restrained from bringing more, because what they already
had was more than enough to do all the work.

Exodus 36:6-7 NIV

Like Moses, we should ask God for clarity in the fullness of
God's vision. Then we should trust God and ask others for the
fullness of provision. God's provision for our ministries comes
through efforts of our asking, trusting, seeking, and gathering in
partnership with God. When we are responding to God's will,
God provides for our needs sufficiently—even abundantly, even
though we may not be able to see it at the time.

Abundance–One Piece at a Time

Throughout his ministry, Jesus repeatedly taught and encouraged
his disciples to trust God's abundance in their lives and in
their ministries. In fact, as Jesus sent out the twelve on their
first mission, he specifically instructed them to trust God's care
instead of their own familiar resources.

He told them to take nothing with them except a walking
stick—no food, no traveler's bag, no money. He told them to
wear sandals but not to take even an extra coat.

Mark 6:8-9 NLT

When the disciples returned from their ministry tour, Jesus encouraged them to come away and rest. But as soon as they began
to leave, a large group started to follow them.

But many people saw them leaving, and people from many
towns ran ahead along the shore and met them as they
landed. A vast crowd was there as he stepped from the boat,
and he had compassion on them because they were like sheep

*without a shepherd. So he taught them many things. Late
in the afternoon his disciples came to him and said, "This is a
desolate place, and it is getting late. Send the crowds away so
they can go to the nearby farms and villages and buy themselves some food." But Jesus said, "You feed them." "With
what?" they asked. "It would take a small fortune to buy
food for all this crowd!" "How much food do you have?" he
asked. "Go and find out." They came back and reported, "We
have five loaves of bread and two fish." Then Jesus told the
crowd to sit down in groups on the green grass. So they sat
in groups of fifty or a hundred. Jesus took the five loaves and
two fish, looked up toward heaven, and asked God's blessing
on the food. Breaking the loaves into pieces, he kept giving
the bread and fish to the disciples to give to the people. They
all ate as much as they wanted, and they picked up twelve
baskets of leftover bread and fish. Five thousand men had
eaten from those five loaves!*

Mark 6:33-44 NLT

In what could have been seen as an obstacle to their rest, Jesus
saw an opportunity to minister to the people who were *like sheep
without a shepherd* needing to be fed

*Our typical scaricity
response is:
"With what?"*

and led. So in response to their spiritual hunger, Jesus fed them the Bread of
Life, the Word of God. But once Jesus
finished teaching, the disciples began
to notice a physical hunger among the
people that was growing more apparent by the moment. But with no obvi-
ous resources available to respond to this need, the disciples saw
only one solution—remove the need by sending the people away.

Jesus saw the people's physical hunger as a great opportunity to
teach the disciples a critical lesson for their ministry: How to
trust God's abundant provision one piece at a time. So instead

of Jesus saying to the disciples, "No problem. I'll feed them," he turned to them and said, "You feed them."

Immediately, the disciples responded to this suggestion with the typical scarcity response: "With what?!" They knew this ministry strategy would require a huge amount of resources, and they figured a quick reality check would reorient Jesus and shut down this strategy. But no, that did not happen.

Jesus had been teaching them about God's full and abundant provision for their Kingdom ministry, and now Jesus saw the hungry crowd before them as the perfect chance to put their teaching into practice. Jesus told the disciples to assess what was available in the way of resources and then to bring to him what they had to offer. So the disciples asked around and gathered what seemed a meager offering, five loaves of bread and two small fish, and brought them to Jesus. Jesus took what was gathered, offered it in prayer to God, and asked God's blessing upon it. Then Jesus instructed the disciples to break down the crowd into more manageable groups to serve. Once the people were grouped, Jesus distributed to the disciples what had been blessed by God one piece at a time. Then the disciples, taking what was given them, fed the huge crowd one person, one group at a time.

We must learn to trust God's provision one piece at a time.

After feeding each group, we can imagine that the disciples had to return to Jesus to receive yet another piece—another part of the full provision which may have seemed barely, if not, enough. And yet each time, with each distribution of the God-blessed resources, it was sufficient for the task. In fact, not only was the provision sufficient, it was abundantly sufficient with twelve baskets of food left over after all the needs—and even wants—were satisfied! However, the disciples (and the crowd being served) did not realize that there was enough until the task was completed and the needs were all met. Instead, they had to trust Jesus for the provision one piece at a time.

So may it be in our ministries. We, like the disciples, when faced with a seemingly impossible mission, must learn to trust God's provision one piece at time. We must ask those around us—even those we are called to serve—what resources they have to offer for the sake of the ministry. We must gather those resources (financial, material, and personnel) and offer those to God for blessing. Additionally, we must break down the seemingly impossible into more manageable service tasks which we can accomplish in a more limited time and space. And then, we must come to God moment by moment, task by task, day by day to receive from God what has been gathered, blessed, and multiplied. Then we must use faithfully what we have been given to accomplish the task at hand, returning to God again each time when more provision is needed.

God's provision is always sufficient—even abundantly sufficient.

In this manner, God's provision will be sufficient, in fact abundantly sufficient. However, we may not realize the abundance until the task is complete. Therefore, we must learn to trust God's abundance even when the provision seems barely, if not, enough.

Manna
One point of great discouragement for many ministries is our fear of not having what we need for the journey. Too many ministries shut down and others never even get off the ground because we cannot see how God will provide for our needs. Imagine how difficult this must have been for Moses and the

Israelites. God called them out of Egypt, painted the picture of the Promised Land, and set them on the journey to claim it. And yet they had not water or food. The people cried out to Moses, and Moses cried out to God. And God answered their prayers (in Exodus 15:22-25) with water and food. Here again, the physical hunger of God's people was the perfect opportunity to demonstrate the fullness and sufficiency of God's provision one piece and one day at a time.

> *The LORD said to Moses, "I will send bread down from heaven like rain. Each day the people can go out and gather only enough for that day. That's how I will see if they obey me."*
> **Exodus 16:4 CEV**

In response to their hunger, God gave them manna, food from heaven, which appeared on the ground each morning. The manna was the perfect food, complete food, which was sufficient for all their nutritional needs, but each day's supply was only good for one day. In fact, if they tried to hoard food for fear of not having enough later, the manna would spoil (Exodus 16:19-20). God tested the people in this to see if they would trust the provision for their needs one day at a time.

Give us today our daily bread.

Jesus taught us that when we pray for God's will we must learn to trust God's provision for it daily:

> *Your Kingdom come, your will be done on earth as it is in heaven. Give us today our daily bread.*
> **Matthew 6:10-11 NIV**

In contrast, if we had all the provision we need for our lives and our ministries up front, our tendency would be to regard the provision as our own, leading us to depend on ourselves or our bank accounts instead of on God. Obviously, God does at times provide for our needs through large gifts and abundant wealth. However, this too requires wise stewardship to honor the provision as coming from God and requires appropriate distribution of these resources one task, one day at a time.

> *To those who use well what they are given, even more will be given. But from those who are unfaithful, even what little they have will be taken away.*
>
> **Luke 19:26 NLT**

We must know and trust the source of all provision, and we must be wise and faithful stewards of the provision as we trust God with it and for it daily.

Avoiding the Bondage of Indebtedness

We have also learned in the world to trust other sources, such as bank loans, to provide for our ministries. However, dependency on loans for our ministry efforts can lead to the bondage of indebtedness and limit our freedom to serve God. Too often we are convinced that indebtedness is the only way to fulfill God's vision for us, so we trust a bank or creditor to provide for the vision instead of trusting God. As a result, when a large portion of our resources is required to pay down the debt, we end up servicing the debt instead of serving God. Jesus warned us about this entrapment when he said:

The bondage of indebtedness can limit our freedom to serve God.

> *You cannot be the slave of two masters! You will like one more than the other or be more loyal to one than the other. You cannot serve both God and money.*
>
> **Matthew 6:24 CEV**

Although a bank loan may not cause us to be disloyal to God, indebtedness can severely restrict our ability to move forward in ministry because we are shackled to money that is owed. Too often, we cannot procure the staff and materials needed to fulfill a ministry when those resources are being used to pay a debt. As a result the ministry can be delayed in moving forward.

Indebtedness can often delay our ministries whereas trusting God's provision may require us to wait. However, we must remember: When we wait on God for pro-vision, the fulfillment of the vision is never delayed.

> ***Slowly, steadily, surely, the time approaches when the vision will be fulfilled. If it seems slow, wait patiently, for it will surely take place. It will not be delayed.***
>
> **Habakkuk 2:3** NLT

Ministry in a Cloud

One of the greatest challenges in ministry is keeping pace with God. We must learn when to move forward with holy boldness and when to wait with patient expectation. But whether we are to move boldly or to wait patiently depends on our following the lead of God.

There will be times in our ministry when everything seems to come together all at once. God's vision for us is clear and the provision is abundant. All the signs are "go," so in obedience, we must move. However, at other times the vision may be blurred, or the provision is just not there. At those times, in obedience, we must wait.

Whether we move boldly or wait patiently depends on our following God.

During times of waiting, we often feel like we have a cloud hanging over our heads or that nothing is being accomplished. However, for the Israelites on their journey to the Promised Land, the cloud was another powerful source of God's provision.

> *The Tabernacle was set up, and on that day the cloud covered it. Then from evening until morning the cloud over the Tabernacle appeared to be a pillar of fire. This was the regular pattern—at night the cloud changed to the appearance of fire. When the cloud lifted from over the sacred tent, the people of Israel followed it. And wherever the cloud settled, the people of Israel camped. In this way, they traveled at the LORD's command and stopped wherever he told them to. Then they remained where they were as long as the cloud stayed over the Tabernacle. If the cloud remained over the Tabernacle for a long time, the Israelites stayed for a long time, just as the LORD commanded. Sometimes the cloud would stay over the Tabernacle for only a few days, so the people would stay for only a few days. Then at the LORD's command they would break camp. Sometimes the cloud stayed only overnight and moved on the next morning. But day or night, when the cloud lifted, the people broke camp and followed. Whether the cloud stayed above the Tabernacle for two days, a month, or a year, the people of Israel stayed in camp and did not move on. But as soon as it lifted, they broke camp and moved on. So they camped or traveled at the LORD's command, and they did whatever the LORD told them through Moses.*
>
> **Numbers 9:15-23** NLT

For the Israelites, the cloud assured them of God's presence, protection, and guidance on their journey, and it clearly told them when to move and when to wait. When the cloud settled over them, the people were to get their households in order and to prepare themselves for what was next on the journey. For when the cloud lifted and moved, the people were to follow readily and immediately without hesitation.

We, too, must learn to accept those times "in the cloud" as precious seasons of preparation when we ready ourselves for where God will take us next. Trusting God to provide clarity in the vision and sufficient resources to fulfill it often requires periods of waiting. However, those times are not necessarily periods of inactivity. Within the cloud, there should be times of rest and Sabbath— of breathing in and being so we will be able to go forth and do. Within the cloud, we should strengthen our relationships with one another so conflict does not distract or detain us when it's time to move. And within the cloud, we should seek clarity regarding the course for our journey and ask for and gather what is needed. But most importantly, we should be assured of God's presence and protection learning to trust God more and more in the cloud.

> *We should accept the times "in the cloud" as precious seasons of preparation.*

On this journey of faith, we are called to discern and submit to the will of God. This allows God to take us where God wants us to go. Therefore, whether we are moving or waiting, we can rest assured that we are where God wants us to be. On the other hand, our refusal to move and refusal to wait are both acts and attitudes of disobedience. The key to obedience in our lives and in our ministries is to *step into the stream* of God's will and stay there following the leading of God.

> *Refusal to move and refusal to wait are both acts and attitudes of disobedience.*

We, as individuals and as the Church, are called to be God's instruments of healing for this broken and hurting world to bring about God's Kingdom on earth. The Kingdom is our ultimate destination, and yet the journey itself is what we are called to complete. The journey did not begin with us, and it will not end with us. Instead, we are called and invited to *step into the stream* of God's will along with a long procession of faithful sojourners who are contending together for the Kingdom of God.

> *And now, may the God of peace, who brought again from the dead our Lord Jesus, equip you with all you need for doing his will. May he produce in you, through the power of Jesus Christ, all that is pleasing to him. Jesus is the Great Shepherd of the sheep by an everlasting covenant signed with his blood. To him be glory forever and ever. Amen.*
>
> **Hebrews 13:20-21 NLT**

Questions for Discussion

1. How can we remain open to the fullness of God's vision for us so we do not limit the ministry or the provision for it?

2. What resources do we need to accomplish specific strategies to live into our vision: personnel (paid or unpaid servants), time (hours per week), space, materials, money?

3. Make a chart noting needs for each prioritized strategy.

4. How can we clearly and faithfully make these needs known to God? To those whom we are serving? To other supporters of this ministry? To members of the ministry team or congregation?

5. How are we willing to wait on God's provision while still moving forward in obedience to the vision?

The Right Next Step as You Live into God's Vision

Over the past several weeks, even months, you have come a long way in the process of discovering God's vision for you and your ministry. And in fact you may now be ready to put God's vision into action. But remember, discernment of and obedience to God's will is an ongoing process that is never truly complete. The journey of discernment is the destination and yet we are blessed to perform as instruments of God's grace along the way.

Continue to meet together for support and accountability along the journey. Continue to dwell with God daily through reading God's word and prayer. God will continue to speak if you continue to listen. Maintain the godly rhythm of breathing in (being) and breathing out (doing.) And assess on a regular basis the needs of your neighbors and your unique ability to respond.

The right next step, then, is to live into God's vision one step, one day at a time trusting God every step along the way.

May God richly bless you and keep you on your journey.

Scripture & Prayers

Day 1
Mark 10: 48-51
Many people told the man to stop, but he shouted even louder, "Son of David, have pity on me!" Jesus stopped and said, "Call him over!" They called out to the blind man and said, "Don't be afraid! Come on! He is calling for you." The man threw off his coat as he jumped up and ran to Jesus. Jesus asked, "What do you want me to do for you?" The blind man answered, "Master, I want to see!" CEV

Jesus, help us continue seeking after you in order that we might know and see the desires you have for us. Give us the boldness to ask but also the awareness of whom we ask. Help us seek you in reverence and mercy. We want to see your desires fulfilled in our midst and your Kingdom glorified and made known. Help us build your Kingdom and not our own. Remind us that you are to be be glorified and made known. Like the blind beggar, we shout more and more, "Lord Jesus, have mercy on us! We want to see!"

Focus Notes

Day 2
Exodus 35:4-5
Moses said to the whole Israelite community, "This is what the Lord has commanded: From what you have, take an offering. Everyone who is willing is to bring to the Lord an offering...."
NIV

Lord, give us willing hearts. Let us give freely to you as you have given freely to us. Convict us to give of our time, our talents, and our possessions. Help us when we ask for support for our ministries to be specific in our asking. Give us clarity in presenting your requests to the people.

Focus Notes

Day 3
2 Kings 4:42-44
A man came from Baal-shalishah, bringing food from the first fruits to the man of God: twenty loaves of barley and fresh ears of grain in his sack. Elisha said, "Give it to the people and let them eat." But his servant said, "How can I set this before a hundred people?" So he repeated, "Give it to the people and let them eat, for thus says the Lord, 'They shall eat and have some left.' He set it before them, they ate, and had some left, according to the word of the Lord. NRSV

Lord, you are sufficient. You make our gifts sufficient when we bring them to you in obedience and with a heart desiring you. Teach us to trust in the Giver and not the gift and in the promise of the future and not the present. You bless our little and make it much. Teach us to rejoice in the small things knowing that you will multiply them into great things for your glory.

Day 4
Philippians 4:19
And this same God who takes care of me will supply all your needs from his glorious riches, which have been given to us in Christ Jesus. NLT

Romans 12:1-2
And so, dear brothers and sisters, I plead with you to give your bodies to God. Let them be a living and holy sacrifice--the kind he will accept. When you think of what he has done for you, is this too much to ask? Don't copy the behavior and customs of this world, but let God transform you into a new person by changing the way you think. Then you will know what God wants you to do, and you will know how good and pleasing and perfect his will really is. NLT

Focus Notes

God, you will fulfill all our needs. Help us know the difference between our needs and our wants. Let us daily seek you and worship you in Spirit and in Truth. Make our will conform to yours. Renew our minds so that we may know and discern your will for us. Then, Lord, we can know that all our needs will be fulfilled.

Day 5
Psalm 78:24-25
He rained down on them manna to eat, and gave them the grain of heaven. Mortals ate of the bread of angels; he sent them food in abundance. NRSV

Focus Notes

God of Grace, help us trust you for our daily provision. Let us not fall into the deception of meeting our own needs. Keep us from becoming slaves to our pride and trusting in those things which fade away and spoil. Help us remember that your gifts are eternal, and are more than we could ever hope or imagine.

Day 6
Psalm 99:7
He spoke to them from the pillar of the cloud; they kept his statutes and the decrees he gave them. NIV

Lord God, teach us to wait and to listen as you protect us in the cloud of your presence. Help us see these times of waiting as times of preparation and focus. Help us be obedient. Help us be still. Help us listen to you. Teach us to remember that in your cloud there is safety, peace and guidance.

Day 7
Ephesians 3:16-21

I pray that from his glorious, unlimited resources he will give you mighty inner strength through his Holy Spirit. And I pray that Christ will be more and more at home in your hearts as you trust in him. May your roots go down deep into the soil of God's marvelous love. And may you have the power to understand, as all God's people should, how wide, how long, how high, and how deep his love really is. May you experience the love of Christ, though it is so great you will never fully understand it. Then you will be filled with the fullness of life and power that comes from God.

Now glory be to God! By his mighty power at work within us, he is able to accomplish infinitely more than we would ever dare to ask or hope. May he be given glory in the church and in Christ Jesus forever and ever through endless ages. Amen. NLT

Jesus, give us the strength to grasp your love even though it is beyond our comprehension. We want to become empty vessels waiting to be filled by you, to be filled with the fullness of God so that we can bring about your Kingdom on earth. You are Lord Jesus. You are the Messiah. Make us willing. Amen

Trust in the Lord
with all your heart;
do not depend
on your own
understanding.
Seek his will
in all you do,
And he will direct
your paths.
Proverbs 3:5-6

Appendix A

Relational Covenants

Please use these sample relational covenants as examples to get you thinking about how to put one together. These are real covenants written by churches and teams working through the material in this book. Feel free to use these in any way that will work for you. New relational covenants can be found at www.steppinginthestream.org.

Local Church # 1
Relational Covenant

As members of the Body of Christ at [Local Church], to protect the integrity of our relationships and ministry, we agree to relate to one another in the following manner:

- To treat one another with Christian LOVE and RESPECT.
- To do and say all things in LOVE for the purpose of building up and never tearing down one another or the church.
- To pray for one another.
- To trust one another.
- To communicate openly by SPEAKING and LISTENING in LOVE.
- To seek HARMONY among each other by TUNING our different voices and opinions to the common pitch of Jesus Christ and His will among us.
- To seek UNITY and not uniformity within the Body of Christ.
- To honor one another's emotions and opinions.

- To commit ourselves to the biblical model of reconciling the differences and hurts among us as prescribed by Jesus Christ in Matthew 18:15-20.
- To seek and trust the good intention and heart of Christ in one another.
- To seek first to understand one another before insisting that we be understood by others.
- To forgive one another as Jesus Christ has forgiven us.

We will hold to the truth in love, becoming more and more in every way like Christ,
who is the head of his body, the Church.
Under his direction, the whole body is fitted together perfectly.
As each part does its own special work,
it helps the other parts grow,
so that the whole body is healthy and growing and full of love.
Ephesians 4:15-16 NLT

Local Church # 2
Relational Covenant

As ones who belong to Jesus Christ and the Body of Christ, we are committed to living out our mission as evidenced in our love for Jesus, one another, and our neighbors. To honor and protect the integrity of our mission and relationships, we commit to relate to one another in the following manner:

- To be honest, open, and forthright with one another as we speak the truth in love.
- To regard one another with humility and kindness as we treat one another as we desire to be treated.

- To do and say all things in love so that our words and actions are encouraging and edifying to one another and the church.
- To honor and respect one another's opinions by listening for the purpose of seeking to understand each other's needs and views—even when we disagree.
- To create the sacred space and time to hear one another's needs, thoughts, and feelings before making important decisions.
- To strive for collaboration on all matters, but be willing to compromise, accommodate, or "let go" when collaboration does not seem possible.
- To seek to understand FIRST God's desires then one another's remembering that ALL our decisions are to build up the Body of Christ and to serve God's purpose.
- To act decisively and to move forward boldly yet humbly once a decision has been made.
- To agree to disagree in love, and when we disagree on major decisions, to not take it personally as we remember that our decisions are to serve God's purpose and not our own.
- To go directly to the person in private who has offended us by following Jesus' process of reconciliation as taught in Matthew 18:15-20.
- To allow for one another's (and the church's) mistakes while holding one another accountable to our purpose and covenant together.
- To forgive one another when we do make mistakes and be willing and able to move on to God's promising future leaving behind the failures and mistakes of the past.

Local Church #3
Relational Covenant

As the Body of Christ at [Local Church],
we acknowledge that God has made each of us as unique
individuals with different gifts, abilities, needs, and opinions, and
that these differences are important and necessary to function as
the Body of Christ *fitted together perfectly... so that the whole body
is healthy and growing and full of love* (Ephesians 4:16).

As we learn to honor and accept one another's differences
and to find where we have true unity,
we commit to:

- Spending time with one another for the purpose of truly getting to know one another.
- Communicating openly as we seek to understand one another's hearts and minds.
- Having the courage to talk directly (one-on-one) to one another when we think we have been wronged or when a disagreement arises.
- Setting our own agenda aside as we seek to reconcile our differences.
- Loving one another and showing compassion in ALL circumstances at ALL times.
- Forgiving one another AND ourselves so we can move forward in our relationships and work together.
- Having faith that we can and will work through ALL issues together .
- Finding healthy closure on all past issues so we can MOVE FORWARD in focusing on what God desires for our church.
- Accepting changes that may be necessary for us to become the church God desires us to be.

- TRUSTING GOD and resting assured that He is in control.

Ministry Team
Relational Covenant

As servants and ambassadors of Jesus Christ, we are called together to equip, nurture, and lead others to be instruments of healing for the Body of Christ. To protect the integrity of our relationships and shared ministry, we commit to:

- Foster among us a culture of encouragement, nurture and support as we respect our differing roles and functions.
- Hold one another accountable to the daily practice of the spiritual and physical disciplines as we seek to grow in God's grace.
- Regard Scripture as our primary plumb line for our lives and our ministry.
- Pray for each other.
- Practice and model all the precepts we teach.
- Adhere to Jesus' process of reconciliation found in Matthew 18:15-20 and refrain from all gossip.
- Forgive and release the other when we fail or disappoint one another.
- Take our work very seriously, but be willing to not always take ourselves too seriously.
- Seek to understand and honor our differences in personalities and in particular how we process information.
- Be proactive and intentional in our communications with each other, especially when anticipating and

encountering any change in our work to help us prepare and respond appropriately to change.

- Embody humility in our relationships and ministry as we submit our will to God's.
- Honor and love one another.
- Tell one another openly when we are in need and what we need in our relationships and ministry.

School or Preschool Staff Relational Covenant

As the faculty and staff of [Local School], to protect and honor our work and relationships together, we commit to:

- Unite around our common goal of educational excellence for all students.
- Embody professionalism and integrity as we become strong examples of all the precepts we teach.
- Treat one another with utmost respect in all we say and do.
- Honor and value the differing experiences, expertise, and views we bring together in caring out our shared mission and goals.
- Support one another fervently especially when faced with personal and professional challenges and communicate clearly any particular needs we have.
- Place the welfare of students first in making decisions regarding our work .
- Value communication as paramount in our work and relationships together by:
  - Communicating clearly any "need to know"

information but not getting distracted by the "want to know" information.

- Practicing discretion regarding staff/faculty issues that should only be addressed in this context.
- Keeping communications positive, focused, and timely.
- Honoring established agendas and meetings to enhance the effectiveness of our time together.

- Release or forgive one another when we have been offended and commit to being reconciled in our differences by:

- Creating an environment that empowers going one-on-one in private when we have been offended.
- Going directly to the other person when there is a concern regarding our work or relationship together.
- Making allowance for one another's mistakes and being accountable for our own mistakes when we make them.

- Honor each staff and faculty as valuable members of our team as we focus on our common mission and goals and not on who gets credit for the results.

Trust in the Lord
with all your heart;
do not depend
on your own
understanding.
Seek his will
in all you do,
And he will direct
your paths.
Proverbs 3:5-6

Appendix B

Spiritual Gifts

Scripture describes spiritual gifts as special abilities given to us for the purpose of serving God and God's people through the Church. All baptized believers have spiritual gifts, and yet we are all gifted differently. No gift is any more special than another, and all gifts are important in fulfilling God's purpose among us. There are many different surveys and inventories to help us assess how God has gifted us through the Holy Spirit. These are available online and through Christian bookstores.

Below are the three primary Scriptural references that describe and list spiritual gifts. No one scripture is all inclusive of all the gifts. However, when we look at these three Scriptures together, a more comprehensive list of gifts emerge. Additionally, various translations may describe the gifts in slightly different manners. Therefore, a comparative listing of the spiritual gifts by Scripture and translation is also included.

Romans 12:6-8

God has given each of us the ability to do certain things well. So if God has given you the ability to prophesy, speak out when you have faith that God is speaking through you. If your gift is that of serving others, serve them well. If you are a teacher, do a good job of teaching. If your gift is to encourage others, do it! If you have money, share it generously. If God has given you leadership ability, take the responsibility seriously. And if you have a gift for showing kindness to others, do it gladly. NLT

We have different gifts, according to the grace given us. If a man's gift is prophesying, let him use it in proportion to his faith. If it is serving, let him serve; if it is teaching, let him teach; if it is encouraging, let him encourage; if it is contributing to the needs of others, let him give generously; if it is leadership, let him govern diligently; if it is showing mercy, let him do it cheerfully. NIV

God has also given each of us different gifts to use. If we can prophesy, we should do it according to the amount of faith we have. If we can serve others, we should serve. If we can teach, we should teach. If we can encourage others, we should encourage them. If we can give, we should be generous. If we are leaders, we should do our best. If we are good to others, we should do it cheerfully. CEV

We have gifts that differ according to the grace given to us: prophecy, in proportion to faith; ministry, in ministering; the teacher, in teaching; the exhorter, in exhortation; the giver, in generosity; the leader, in diligence; the compassionate, in cheerfulness. NRSV

I Corinthians 12:7-11

The Spirit has given each of us a special way of serving others. Some of us can speak with wisdom, while others can speak with knowledge, but these gifts come from the same Spirit. To others the Spirit has given great faith or the power to heal the sick 10or the power to work mighty miracles. Some of us are prophets, and some of us recognize when God's Spirit is present. Others can speak different kinds of languages, and still others can tell what these languages mean. But it is the Spirit who does all this and decides which gifts to give to each of us. CEV

Now to each one the manifestation of the Spirit is given for the common good. To one there is given through the Spirit the message of wisdom, to another the message of knowledge by means of the same Spirit, to another faith by the same Spirit, to another gifts of healing by that one Spirit, to another miraculous powers, to another prophecy, to another distinguishing between spirits, to another speaking in different kinds of tongues, and to still another the interpretation of tongues. All these are the work of one and the same Spirit, and he gives them to each one, just as he determines. NIV

A spiritual gift is given to each of us as a means of helping the entire church. To one person the Spirit gives the ability to give wise advice; to another he gives the gift of special knowledge. The Spirit gives special faith to another, and to someone else he gives the power to heal the sick. He gives one person the power to perform miracles, and to another the ability to prophesy. He gives someone else the ability to know whether it is really the Spirit of God or another spirit that is speaking. Still another person is given the ability to speak in unknown languages, and another is given the ability to interpret what is being said. It is the one and only Holy Spirit who distributes these gifts. He alone decides which gift each person should have. NLT

To each is given the manifestation of the Spirit for the common good. To one is given through the Spirit the utterance of wisdom, and to another the utterance of knowledge according to the same Spirit, to another faith by the same Spirit, to another gifts of healing by the one Spirit, to another the working of miracles, to another prophecy, to another the discernment of spirits, to another various kinds of tongues, to another the interpretation of tongues. All these are activated by one and the same Spirit, who allots to each one individually just as the Spirit chooses. NRSV

Ephesians 4:11-13

Christ chose some of us to be apostles, prophets, missionaries, pastors, and teachers, so that his people would learn to serve and his body would grow strong. This will continue until we are united by our faith and by our understanding of the Son of God. Then we will be mature, just as Christ is, and we will be completely like him. CEV

It was he who gave some to be apostles, some to be prophets, some to be evangelists, and some to be pastors and teachers, to prepare God's people for works of service, so that the body of Christ may be built up until we all reach unity in the faith and in the knowledge of the Son of God and become mature, attaining to the whole measure of the fullness of Christ. NIV

He is the one who gave these gifts to the church: the apostles, the prophets, the evangelists, and the pastors and teachers. Their responsibility is to equip God's people to do his work and build up the church, the body of Christ, until we come to such unity in our faith and knowledge of God's Son that we will be mature and full grown in the Lord, measuring up to the full stature of Christ. NLT

The gifts he gave were that some would be apostles, some prophets, some evangelists, some pastors and teachers, to equip the saints for the work of ministry, for building up the body of Christ, until all of us come to the unity of the faith and of the knowledge of the Son of God, to maturity, to the measure of the full stature of Christ. NRSV

List of Spiritual Gifts by Scripture and Translation

Romans 12

CEV	NIV	NLT	NRSV
Prophesy	Prophesy	Prophesy	Prophesy
Service	Service	Service	Ministry
Teaching	Teaching	Teaching	Teaching
Encouragement	Encouragement	Encouragement	Exhortation
Giving	Giving	Giving	Giving
Leadership	Leadership	Leadership	Leadership
Kindness	Mercy	Kindness	Compassion

1 Corinthians 12

Wisdom	Wisdom	Wisdom	Wisdom
Knowledge	Knowledge	Knowledge	Knowledge
Faith	Faith	Faith	Faith
Healing	Healing	Healing	Healing
Miracles	Miracles	Miracles	Miracles
Prophets	Prophecy	Prophecy	Prophecy
Discernment	Discernment	Discernment	Discernment
Languages	Tongues	Unknown languages	Tongues
Interpretation	Interpretation	Interpretation	Interpretation

Ephesians 4

Apostle	Apostle	Apostle	Apostle
Prophet	Prophet	Prophet	Prophet
Missionary	Evangelist	Evangelist	Evangelist
Pastor	Pastor	Pastor	Pastor
Teacher	Teacher	Teacher	Teacher

List of Spiritual Gifts

Romans 12: 6-8
1 Corinthians 12:7-11
Ephesians 4:11-13

Apostleship

Discernment

Encouragement

Evangelism

Faith

Giving

Healing

Interpretation

Kindness

Knowledge

Leadership

Miracles

Pastoring

Prophecy

Serving

Speaking in Tongues

Teaching

Wisdom

Bibliography

Anderson, Neil T. *Victory Over Darkness*. Regal Books: Ventura, California, 2000.

Barna, George. *Turning Vision Into Action*. Regal Books: Ventura, California, 1996.

Bonhoeffer, Dietrich. *The Cost of Discipleship*. Macmillan Company: New York, 1966.

Reman, Rachel Naomi. *Kitchen Table Wisdom*. Riverhead Books: New York, 1996.

United Methodist Hymnal. United Methodist Publishing House: Nashville, Tennessee, 1989.

Wesley, John. *Explanatory Notes on the New Testament*.

PLOWPOINT

Breaking Ground for the Seed of the Gospel

• Mission

Breaking ground for the seed of the Gospel through ministries
that prepare and repair the Church and church leaders.

• Vision

The Church prepared and repaired for ministry by becoming
an effective instrument of healing for the broken and hurting world.

• Ministry Strategies

Congregational Services

To equip and empower the local church and church leaders to respond effectively and
obediently to God's call for them.
• Longing to Belong
Relational healing/conflict resolution.
• Stepping in the Stream
Strategic discernment and implementation of God's vision.
Staff and Leadership Development

Shepherd Care

Holistic, year-long wellness program for clergy to equip, empower, and nurture
pastors to be effective and obedient shepherds of the flock by strengthening their
spiritual, physical, and emotional health.

Resource Development

To equip and empower the local church and church leaders to fulfill God's purpose
among them through biblically based materials and resources.

Sanctuary

A sacred space for equpping, nurturing, healing and releasing church leaders in a
sacred environment immersed in worship and intercession.

Plowpoint, an extension ministry in the Western North Carolina Conference of the United Methodist
Church, is incorparated as a non-profit ministry in the state of North Carolina and is recognized by the
IRS as a 501(c)(3) organization.

Plowpoint Resources

Resources Available

- *Longing to Belong: learning to relate as the body of Christ*
  A ten week study designed to equip the church and church leaders to respond to conflict while strengthening our relationships with Jesus Christ and one another.
  Book, Videotape and DVD and Facilitator's Guide available.
- *Feeding and Leading of Shepherds: learning to relate as Sheep and Shepherds.*
  Designed to reclaim and strengthen the biblical call and ministry of spiritual leaders as shepherds of the flock.
- *Stepping in the Stream: learning to relate to the will of God.* A guide for individual, congregational, and ministry team discernment of God's vision with practical "next steps" to put the vision into action.

Easy Ways to Order

Fill out the form below with your name, address, phone numbers, email and the resources you want to order. Send it in by any of the means listed here:

PO Box 979 Graham NC 27253
Phone: 336-226-0282 Fax: 336-226-5894
resources@plowpoint.org
www.plowpoint.org

Name:
Address:
City, State, ZIP
Phone Number:
Email:
Please send me the following: